NORTH-WEST HIGHLANDS

Norman Newton

D&C

David and Charles

D1335728

Right: Knoydart – looking over Loch Hourn
towards Beinn Sgritheall (John Cleare).

CONTENTS

INTRODUCING THE NORTH-WEST HIGHLANDS

T HE NORTH-WEST HIGHLANDS OF SCOTLAND – an area of outstanding natural beauty, and harrowing human history – appeals to a wide range of visitors and has been a destination for tourists and 'excursionists' for over two hundred years. The land of the mountain and the flood, celebrated in verse and song by generations of exiles since the middle of the eighteenth century, it can be almost painfully beautiful or cruelly demanding – sometimes on the same day. The scenery of the Highlands is justifiably famous throughout the world: there are few places with such a range of natural beauty, with some of the oldest rocks in the world ranged alongside more recent volcanic landscapes, all subject to the processes of glaciation during the last Ice Age. The present landscape is not always a 'natural' wilderness, but sometimes man-made, whether by the early agriculturalists of the Neolithic period and the Bronze Age, or more recently due to overgrazing by the sheep and cattle which replaced most of the human inhabitants in the nineteenth century.

The history of the Highlands is long and bloody, and there are reminders everywhere in the form of ruined castles and historic monuments dating from the Viking period and the Middle Ages to the poignant war memorials of the twentieth century. The Highlands have been occupied many times, notably by Norse invaders and settlers (AD800-1150), by Anglo-Norman invaders who settled in the fertile Lowlands and the coastal plains of the Highlands in the eleventh and twelfth centuries, by Cromwellian forces during the civil wars of the seventeenth century, and by troops representing the Hanoverian government of Great Britain after the Jacobite risings of 1715 and 1745.

Sometimes the invaders were not military men: in the nineteenth century many Highland lairds (landowners) evicted the local population from their farms and cottages and replaced them with Lowland shepherds, brought into the glens to run the vast flocks of sheep which were far more profitable than people. The process known as 'The Highland Clearances' began in the last years of the eighteenth century, but reached its peak in the middle of the nineteenth century, by when many thousands of Highlanders had emigrated, either by choice or by force, to the new colonies in North America,

Looking over the picturesque village of Plockton on Loch Carron to the entrance of Loch Kishorn, with the mountains of Applecross and Torridon behind

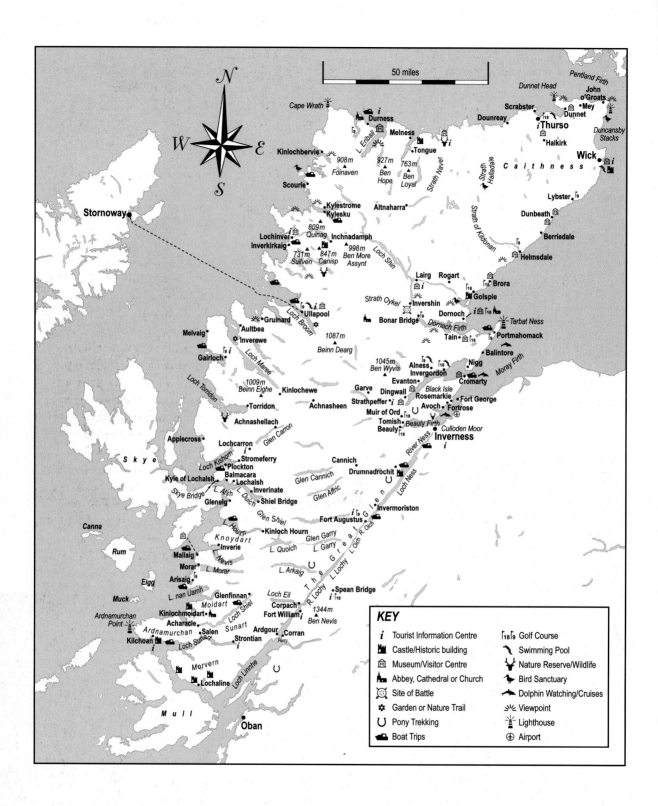

KEY

i	Tourist Information Centre	⌐18 ⌐9	Golf Course
🏰	Castle/Historic building		Swimming Pool
🏛	Museum/Visitor Centre		Nature Reserve/Wildlife
	Abbey, Cathedral or Church		Bird Sanctuary
	Site of Battle		Dolphin Watching/Cruises
✿	Garden or Nature Trail		Viewpoint
U	Pony Trekking		Lighthouse
	Boat Trips	⊕	Airport

Australia and New Zealand. Each summer their descendants return, keen to trace their ancestry and find their roots.

Until the late nineteenth century, most Highlanders were Gaelic-speaking, and immersed in Gaelic culture. Today, Gaelic speakers number certainly less than a hundred thousand out of a Scottish population of over five million. Perhaps only half that number are native speakers, and many of them now live in Scotland's cities. Gaelic is strongest in the Outer Hebrides and on the island of Skye. Only a few hundred native speakers are left on the Highland mainland; many of them reside in Inverness. Despite these statistics, Gaelic is fighting vigorously for survival, and many talented people promote the cause. One of the most obvious signs of Gaelic culture is in the place-names of the Highlands, though along the west coast, and in the Islands, most of the place-names are Gaelic versions of Norse names, fixed firmly in the landscape during the 350 years of Norse occupation, starting around AD800.

In this book, 'the north-west Highlands' means the area of Scotland north and west of the Great Glen, that great geological gash and rift valley which slashes through the Highlands at an angle, from Inverness at its north-eastern end to Fort William in the south-west. Thus, the north-west Highlands extends from Caithness and Sutherland in the north to Lochaber and Morvern in the south, and from the mountain fastnesses of

TRAVEL IN THE HIGHLANDS

Getting around the Highlands is much easier than it used to be. Fast, modern roads connect the major centres of population, and Inverness is linked to the south by the new, improved, realigned and widened A9, the major trunk road through the middle of Scotland. There is an overnight sleeper train from London to Inverness and Fort William, and onward rail connections from Inverness to Kyle of Lochalsh, Wick and Thurso. There are airports at Wick and at Dalcross, east of Inverness, with links to Orkney, Shetland, Stornoway, Aberdeen, Glasgow, Edinburgh and London.

However, there are still many miles of single-track roads in the Highlands, and some advice to the traveller will avoid problems. Passing places are provided at frequent intervals, and motorists are urged to use these courteously, to allow oncoming traffic to pass, and to allow following traffic to overtake. When using passing places, always stop on the left side of the road.

The Skye ferry leaving Mallaig for Armadale (Author)

ENJOYING THE OUTDOORS

If hill-walking, dress for all weathers, and wear stout footwear. Wellies are positively dangerous in wet conditions on the hills and should be reserved for wading. Always take a map and compass, and know how to use them. Most Scots regard access to the hills as a non-negotiable birthright, but foreign landowners do not always agree, so it pays to take local advice. In the shooting season, it is only common sense to enquire locally to see if there are any shooters in the hills. And then, of course, there are the midges! They are a menace, and unrelenting. Various commercial potions claim to repel them, but on a midgey day the best thing is to avoid them, by staying away from damp, dark, sheltered areas. When the midges are at their worst, the best place for a picnic is on the most windswept site you can find, preferably in the sunshine, which is not as rare in the Highlands as some would have you believe.

Pages 10–11: Looking west from Strathy Point, on the north coast of Sutherland

Right: Thrift and roseroot on the Point of Ardnamurchan

Opposite: Loch Stack and Arkle, near Laxford Bridge in north-west Sutherland

Pages 14–15: Eilean Donan Castle on Loch Duich

Torridon in the west to the capital of the Highlands, Inverness, on its eastern boundary. This includes parts of the old counties of Caithness, Sutherland, Ross and Cromarty, Inverness-shire and Argyll. The history of local government in the Highlands is complicated, but important to people researching family history, who need to know which parish their ancestors lived in.

The natural history of the Highlands can never be taken for granted, and constantly surprises with its range and complexity; a tremendous diversity of habitats and ecosystems can occur in a comparatively small area. The flora and fauna which inhabit our scenic landscapes are rich, varied, unusual and often rare. In only a few miles, habitats can vary from sheltered, lush coastal pockets through sloping hillsides of birch, oak and hazel, to peat bogs and moorland, and finally to alpine species. Small wonder the area is so popular with botanists, from specialists in mosses and lichens to the conservators of the ancient Caledonian pine forest. In August the hills burst into colour, as the purple heather blooms, but throughout the year there are natural pleasures to enjoy. In spring, wildflowers turn the coastal machair (coastal grasslands) into a tapestry of colour, while the yellow of gorse and broom can be seen in any month.

The range of bird life is equally broad, and visitors are amazed to see how prolific it is: the crossbill and the capercaillie, superbly adapted to life in the pine forest, grouse, denizen of the higher ground, ospreys and sea-eagles, kestrels, falcons and buzzards, and of course the golden eagles which soar above the highest mountains and craggiest terrains.

While the animals of the Highlands are not as prolific as they once were – the brown bear disappeared by the tenth century AD, while in later centuries the beaver, wild boar and wolf were hunted to extinction – foxes, pine martens, badgers and red deer survive in large numbers, while around the coasts, otters and two species of seals are thriving.

Finally, respect both the people and the landscape of the Highlands. You will find here hospitality and friendliness unmatched anywhere else in the British Isles. This book gives you some ideas, in words and pictures, of where to go in the north-west Highlands for the best scenery and the most interesting history, but the best way to explore the Highlands is to equip yourself with plenty of time, and prepare to wander.

1 INVERNESS, THE BLACK ISLE AND EASTER ROSS

INVERNESS

THE TOWN OF INVERNESS is variously described as 'the capital of the Highlands', 'the Hub of the Highlands' and 'the Gateway to the Highlands'. It is all of these, and also home to a population now exceeding 50,000.

Inverness in the 1950s was a small Scottish provincial town with a population of 28,000, but over the last fifty years it has grown continuously and it will not be long before it has doubled in size from the Highland capital of the postwar years. New housing estates have spread up the lower slopes of the prehistoric hill fort of Craig Phadraig to the west and on the sloping hills along the River Ness to the south, but most of the expansion has been to the east, where the tiny villages and townships of Cradlehall, Smithton, Culloden and Balloch have been transformed into suburbs.

Inverness is a busy, modern town, with a full range of services and facilities for both residents and visitors. Sadly, the historic heart of the town was swept away in the 1960s in the name of progress, much to the regret of native Invernessians. Almost nothing remains of medieval Inverness, apart from a couple of buildings on Church Street. The Town House, an example of late-Victorian architectural extravagance, is the most impressive building remaining.

Beside the Town House is Inverness Museum, where the archaeology and natural history of the area are displayed and explained. There is a café and a museum shop. The museum has an important collection of Jacobite material, and a small art gallery and exhibition space on the top floor. The Tourist Information Centre is located on the ground floor of the museum building.

Inverness, the capital of the Highlands

RECREATION IN INVERNESS

Many of the sports and leisure facilities of Inverness are situated in the Bught area of the town, on the banks of the Ness south of Eden Court Theatre. There are running tracks, sports pitches, the Aquadome and Sports Centre – excellent facilities for a rainy day. In the same area is the impressive Floral Hall, operated by the local authority, Highland Council. Eden Court Theatre is important in the cultural life of the town, enjoying widespread support not just from the local townsfolk but from the scattered population of the Highlands. Booking is advisable, especially for the infrequent but eagerly anticipated visits by national companies.

Balnain House – 'The Home of Highland Music', where the history of the classical music of Gaelic culture, pibroch bagpipe music, is explained – is on the west bank of the Ness, opposite the town centre, at the west end of the Greig Street iron suspension bridge. Balnain House was built in the eighteenth century, then requisitioned by the government after the Battle of Culloden (1746) as the headquarters of Roy's Military Survey of Scotland in the north. From here teams of surveyors went out and created a marvellous (and top-secret) map of the Highlands, to be used by troops in the event of future risings by the Jacobite clans. It was never needed for military purposes but became a wonderful source for local historians and genealogists. Balnain House was rescued from dereliction and restored to its present state in the 1990s. It contains an excellent café and a shop where all sorts of Highland and Scottish music can be purchased, as well as instruments on which to play that music. It is well worth a visit – the exhibitions and displays are of superb quality.

Inverness Museum and Balnain House are perfect for giving a good general introduction to the history, culture and natural environment of the Highlands, but many visitors may well have a more personal interest in the area. It is often reckoned that there may be 25 million people of Highland descent in North America alone, many of whose ancestors left their native land in the emigrations of the eighteenth and nineteenth centuries.

Inverness Public Library, located in the centre of town beside the bus station at Farraline Park, has an excellent collection of books on Highland history and culture. Much of the history of the Highlands is contained in local newspapers which are available for consultation in the library on microfilm, with indexes by both subjects and personal names for the period 1809-1900.

For those interested in researching their family tree, Highland Archives, located in the same building as the public library in Inverness, holds census records on microfilm for all Highland parishes, every ten years from 1841 to 1891. The records for 1901 will become available in 2001. There are also Old Parish Registers of births, baptisms, marriages and deaths, as well as the *International Genealogical Index* compiled by the Mormon church. Increasingly, genealogical records are available electronically on the Internet, but there is no substitute for the knowledge and expertise of the full-time genealogist employed by Highland Archives. Bookings are essential, and during the busy summer season you are quite likely to meet a distant relative – or at least somebody with the same clan name – in the library's reference room where the genealogist's consultations are held and where the family history records are kept.

Inverness has a long history as a royal burgh, though in the Middle Ages it competed with other towns in the north for the position of supremacy it has achieved today. Strategically Inverness was always the key to maintaining control of the Highlands and so the whole of the north of Scotland, and over the centuries it has been taken and retaken numerous times by competing forces. Inverness Castle was originally built to guard the crucial crossing of the River Ness – though the buildings you see today were built in the nineteenth century as a prison and courthouse.

In front of Inverness Castle stands a statue of Flora MacDonald, looking down the Great Glen for her prince, her faithful dog beside her. It was she who famously assisted Charles Edward Stuart – 'Bonnie Prince Charlie' – disguised as a female domestic servant to escape from government troops pursuing him through the Hebrides after the Battle of Culloden in 1746. After many adventures, including a spell in North America during the Revolutionary War, Flora MacDonald returned to her native Isle of Skye and is buried there, in the cemetery at Kilmuir. The Inverness statue was unveiled in 1899 in front of a crowd of several thousands, with the provost, town council, magistrates, town clerk and other officials and dignitaries in attendance.

Flora MacDonald is photographed by thousands of tourists every year – the plaque on her pedestal quotes the famous lines from Dr Johnson:

... a name that will be mentioned in history, and if courage and fidelity be virtues, mentioned with honour.

On two notable occasions Inverness found itself involved in conflicts which affected the course of Scottish history. In 1411 Donald of the Isles, Lord of the Isles and Earl of Ross, arrived at the town at the head of a massive army of Highlanders and Islanders. They burnt the famous wooden bridge across the Ness below the castle and sacked the town. The burghers of Inverness offered little resistance, though one man, John Cumming, put on his armour and head-piece, took up his two-handed sword, and stood at the end of the town bridge to defy the might of the MacDonald and his armies. It was said that had there been ten men as brave as John Cumming in Inverness, neither the bridge nor the town would have been destroyed.

Donald of the Isles went on to fight one of the great set-piece battles of Scottish history. His failure to win decisively at the Battle of Harlaw, where his Highland army met the forces of the Scottish crown near Aberdeen, ensured that the dominance of the Scottish state, and the decline of Gaelic-speaking chieftains, would inevitably place Highland culture and Highland people under continuous and increasing pressure.

These historical processes reached their seemingly inevitable conclusion on 16 April 1746 on Drumossie Muir, just outside Inverness. The Battle of Culloden ended Bonnie Prince Charlie's Jacobite rising of 1745-6 . Although

Above: The statue of Flora MacDonald stands in front of the courthouse in Inverness; she is looking down the Great Glen for her prince

Opposite: Inverness Castle, a nineteenth-century courthouse and prison, built on the site of the medieval stronghold destroyed by the Jacobites in 1746; the flag shows that the High Court is in session

the battle was fought just up the hill from Culloden House, on what is now called Culloden Moor, this was a battle for the control of Inverness. The carnage of the day was dreadful; the cruelty of the successful government troops afterwards was terrible, even by the standards of the time.

The Culloden battlefield, situated 6 miles (10km) east of Inverness off the main A96 Aberdeen road, is now in the care of the National Trust for Scotland. The battle lines of the opposing armies are marked with coloured standards; the burial stones of several Highland clans bear silent witness to the carnage. A large cairn commemorates the battle, and here the Gaelic Society of Inverness holds a memorial service every April.

Inverness is not only the cultural and historical 'Hub of the Highlands' but also lies at the hub of an extensive transport network. Roads radiate out from Inverness to all points of the compass, while the vastly improved A9 road links the Highland capital to Perth, that other 'Gateway to the Highlands', and so to Glasgow, Edinburgh and the south. The A9 is a dual carriageway for long stretches, but some sections are dangerous and many accidents result from speeding and careless driving. Foreign tourists seem to be especially vulnerable. Please drive carefully and allow ample time for your journey as both busy traffic in the summer and adverse weather conditions in winter can render the journey longer than expected. Three hours is the normal journey time to Inverness from Edinburgh or Glasgow.

The coming of the railway to Inverness in the 1860s assured the town's growth and prosperity; fortunately the Highland rail network survived the depredations of Dr Beeching in the 1960s. Inverness is linked to London by a popular overnight sleeper service and several trains travel daily to Glasgow, Edinburgh, Aberdeen and London. Other services link Inverness to Kyle of Lochalsh (for Skye), and to Wick and Thurso (for Orkney). The train journey to Inverness from Glasgow or Edinburgh takes about three-and-a-half hours. Dalcross Airport, lately enlarged and improved, has air links to London, Stornoway and other Scottish airports. The journey from London takes about an hour and a half.

Inverness is thus easy to get to and makes an excellent base from which to explore the Highlands further. Most of the territory described in this book can be reached in day trips from the Highland capital – but we advise a more leisurely approach to travelling in the Highlands.

THE COMPLEXITIES OF CULLODEN

Adjoining the Culloden battlefield is an NTS visitor centre, beside some farm steadings thought to date from the time of the battle. The NTS exhibition is interesting and informative, stressing the fact that Culloden should not be seen as an England versus Scotland encounter – Scottish troops, including Highlanders (Campbells) fought on the government side, while soldiers from both France and Ireland fought for the Jacobites. Many Lowlanders fought with Bonnie Prince Charlie, and more Highlanders signed up with the Hanoverian government's 'Independent Companies' than supported the Jacobites, though they were kept away from the battle at Culloden. The politics of the time are complicated and historical research throws up many surprises. Visitors seeking to investigate these matters further will find an excellent bookshop at Culloden, along with a gift shop and restaurant.

THE BLACK ISLE

To the north of Inverness, across the new Kessock Bridge (1982) which carries the A9 across the Beauly Firth, is the Black Isle, which is not an island and is not black! It used to be a bit of a backwater, very traditional, passed-by by most of the modern world. However, the new bridge, replacing the extremely leisurely Kessock Ferry, has made the southern shore of the Black Isle into a suburb of Inverness and brought the rest of it

Opposite: Kessock Bridge spans the narrows of the Moray Firth to link Inverness to the Black Isle and the North (John Cleare)

HILL FORTS

Throughout the Highlands of Scotland many strategic hilltops are occupied by prehistoric forts, built in the Iron Age to protect local tribes and local chieftains from military threats – both from 'foreign' invaders and from each other. They come in various styles, but usually there are one or more drystone walls circling the summit of a prominent hill, overlooking the entrance to a Highland glen, an important river crossing, or an ancient tribal boundary.

Most extraordinary are the 'vitrified' hill forts, so called because the stone of the ramparts has been melted by incredibly high temperatures and has become glassy, often because of silica in the local rocks. Once thought to be a deliberate construction technique to strengthen the ramparts, this phenomenon is now recognised as the result either of fires set against the walls by attackers, or of accidental destruction fanned by high winds.

Most hill forts are thought to date from around 1000-750BC.

Opposite: The 'Clootie Well' near Avoch, on the Black Isle

within commuting distance. The full effect of the new bridge has been but slowly appreciated – even Dingwall, the county town of Ross and Cromarty, is now barely twenty minutes from Inverness.

The Black Isle is a peninsula, with the Cromarty Firth on one side and the Beauly and Moray Firths on the other. The villages of Beauly and Muir of Ord occupy the thick neck of land which links it to the rest of the mainland. From out at sea the central ridge of the peninsula has a dark appearance from which perhaps the name is derived. By the middle of the nineteenth century most of the peat on that ridge had been cut for fuel for the hearths of Fortrose, Rosemarkie and Cromarty, but before that it would have seemed even darker than it does today, especially in winter.

Crossing the Kessock Bridge, there are fine views eastwards to Fortrose and Fort George, and westwards to Inverness and the Beauly Firth. The North Kessock Tourist Information Centre, on the A9 at the north end of the bridge, is a good place to stop and walk back to admire the view. Straight ahead is the Ord Hill, surmounted by a prehistoric vitrified hill fort, guarding this strategically important narrows. Looking back across the Beauly Firth to Inverness the comparable hill fort of Craig Phadraig is clearly visible, with the cemetery hill of Tomnahurich arising out of the housing estates of Inverness.

Travelling north from Inverness, the first village encountered on the Black Isle is North Kessock. Apart from the new housing estates there is an old-fashioned hotel with excellent traditional pub food and, across the road from the hotel, a viewpoint where the comings and goings of the Moray Firth dolphins, and of the pleasure craft which follow them, can be observed. Different companies run 'dolphin tours' from the pier at North Kessock and from Inverness Harbour.

The little settlement of Kilmuir, just around the corner from the Kessock Bridge but reached by road by a more circuitous route, has a medieval church.

Continuing up the east side of the Black Isle the road reaches Munlochy Bay with the settlements of Munlochy and Avoch at its head. For reasons to do with Gaelic orthography the first two letters of 'Avoch' are not pronounced, so it is known locally as 'Och'. Wags observe that much 'patience' is required to live here – Patience is a common surname in this little fishing village. There is a local museum and an active local-history group which puts on exhibitions and publishes books and leaflets of local interest.

The most famous son of Avoch is Alexander Mackenzie, one of the explorers who helped to open up the western wildernesses of Canada to Victorian 'civilisation'. The Mackenzie River is named after him. He is a great cultural hero in Canada and many Canadians make their way to Avoch to view his monument.

There are two 'clootie wells' in this area – one beside the road to Avoch – where the traditional practice of visiting on the first Sunday in May, preferably at sunrise, to partake of the sacred waters and to hang a piece of

THE BRAHAN SEER

It was at Chanonry Point that Coinneach Odhar, the 'Brahan Seer', was burned in a tar barrel for witchcraft. His 'prophecies' were written up and published by Alexander Mackenzie in 1877. Modern scholars and historians have difficulty reconciling the many tales associated with the Brahan Seer with the historical record. Of more interest is the way in which the stories shed light on the culture and folk beliefs of the society which produced them.

cloth ('cloot') on one of the surrounding trees, in the hope of an efficacious outcome, is still followed religiously.

The village of Fortrose has been a royal burgh since 1590 but is famed today for its ruined cathedral, dating from the middle of the thirteenth century, and its academy, consistently recognised as one of the best secondary schools in the Highlands. One of the Lords of the Isles issued charters from Fortrose and is reportedly buried there, by virtue of his entitlement (through marriage) to the Earldom of Ross. The old lighthouse on Chanonry Point is another good spot for viewing dolphins. The point takes its name from the old name for Fortrose. From here the stone cliffs of Fort George are clearly visible across the narrows, one of the Hanoverian fortresses built to 'pacify' the Highlands after the Jacobite risings in the eighteenth century.

Before the medieval cathedral of Fortrose was built the local monastic site was a mile further north, at Rosemarkie, now a tiny village but the site of one of the outstanding museums and tourist attractions in the north of Scotland – Groam House Museum. This little gem of a museum is dedicated primarily to the Picts and their strange symbol stones and crosses, of which a superb example was found locally and is now well displayed. The museum has a well-stocked little bookshop and also an excellent research collection of materials relating to the study of the Picts – an enigmatic people who were the dominant cultural group

in these parts for most of the first millennium AD.

Visitors with an interest in ecclesiastical history may also be interested in the Valliscaulian priory at Beauly, founded in 1230 by French monks. Beauly is located in the 'neck' of the Black Isle peninsula and derives its name from the French *beau lieu*, 'beautiful place'. Nearby is the ancestral home of the Frasers of Lovat, Beaufort Castle, sold in the 1990s along with most of their estates to pay off massive debts.

The principal town of the Black Isle is Cromarty, at its northern tip. This village is an attractive time capsule of eighteenth-century Scottish town architecture, with many interesting nooks and crannies, including an ice house and a former rope factory. The little harbour looks across the narrow entrance to the Cromarty Firth to the Hill of Nigg and the oil-rig construction yard nearby. The two headlands guarding this important anchorage are known as 'the Sutors of Cromarty'.

Above: Detail of a memorial to Sir Alexander Mackenzie in Fortrose Cathedral

Opposite: Fortrose Cathedral; built in the thirteenth century, the stones of its ruins were used to build Cromwell's Fort in Inverness

Pages 26–7: The view from the vitrified hill fort of Knock Farrell, looking across Strath Peffer to Ben Wyvis

Until the middle of the nineteenth century Cromarty and Inverness competed as royal burghs for trade and for the reputation as the best port and anchorage in the north. But with the coming of the railway, Inverness prospered and Cromarty stagnated. However, whereas in Inverness only a handful of older buildings survive, in Cromarty the eighteenth-century town is largely intact and is now a conservation area.

The history of Cromarty is recounted in Cromarty Courthouse, a handsome Georgian building finished in 1783 and now converted for use as a museum and heritage centre, with animated models recreating a trial. One room is dedicated to Sir Thomas Urquhart (1611-60), writer, philosopher, linguist and professional eccentric. This Laird of Cromarty attempted to invent a universal language which reads as well backwards as forwards, offered a new theory of trigonometry, was imprisoned by Cromwell for being too ardent a royalist and supposedly died of an uncontrollable fit of laughter on hearing of the Restoration of Charles II.

One of the few seventeenth-century buildings in Cromarty is the cottage which belonged to Hugh Miller (1802-56), the Cromarty stone mason who taught himself geology and journalism and was one of the best-known personalities in nineteenth-century Scotland. He shot himself on Christmas Eve 1856, unable to reconcile his scientific observations with the creation story of the Book of Genesis. Other early geologists, with whom Miller corresponded, insisted correctly on the great age of the earth's rocks, while Miller strove too literally to reconcile the new knowledge with the Bible. Eventually he was no longer able to sustain his position. He was a complex man, with a dark, moody and detached personality. The museum in his cottage contains much interesting material, including many fossils.

THE PICTS

Their name Picti, *'the painted ones', was perhaps bestowed as a nickname by somebody in a Roman garrison in Scotland around AD300, but the Picts had always been there – they are the descendants of the original inhabitants of what became 'Scotland'. They possessed the art of writing but have left no written records, just mysterious symbols carved on dozens of stones. They occupied at one time the whole of the northern half of Scotland, including the Northern Isles and the Hebrides, but with the densest concentration in Aberdeenshire and Strathmore and around the Moray Firth.*

The precise meaning of the symbol-stones is elusive but this has not deterred scholars from speculation. Amongst the most common symbols are a 'mirror', comb, crescent, 'Z-rod', various animals including a horse, goose, eagle, salmon, and boar, and the enigmatic 'swimming beast' which sometimes looks a little like a dolphin.

The Picts disappear from history around AD850, perhaps as the result of Viking pressure on the colony of Scotti *in Argyll, whose leadership intermarried with the Pictish matriarchy and perhaps conquered the Picts by military force. The recognition of the ruler of Dalriada Kenneth MacAlpin as King of the Picts in AD843 is taken as a symbolic event creating the Kingdom of Scotland.*

EASTER ROSS

The villages of Easter Ross – Alness, Evanton, Invergordon and Tain – are all now by-passed by the new, improved A9 road, which zooms across the Black Isle, across the Cromarty Firth, and almost before you know it, across the Dornoch Firth and into Sutherland. Yet these villages are all worth a visit; all have their individuality and their own attractions.

At the south end of the Cromarty Firth is the town of Dingwall with its craft shops and pedestrianised precincts, its civic architecture and statuary a nostalgic reminder that it was once the county town of Ross and Cromarty. It's quieter today, but worth exploring. With a population of only 5,000 Dingwall is proud of its long history. The name is Norse, suggesting an administrative centre where a Norse assembly once met, as at Tingwall in Shetland or Tynwald on the Isle of Man.

Dingwall was made a royal burgh in 1226 and once had an important castle, of which only slight traces remain. The Tolbooth dates from 1730 and houses a small museum. Tulloch Castle, formerly the seat of the Davidsons, is now a conference centre. Overlooking the town is a prominent tower in the local cemetery, commemorating General Sir Hector MacDonald, a local crofter's son who through military prowess gained the title 'Fighting Mac'. He served in Afghanistan, Egypt and the Sudan, covering himself with glory and worshipped by his men. He shot himself in a Paris hotel room in 1903, following allegations about his private life, involving small boys in Ceylon. The details were hushed up at the time and local people refused to entertain any suggestion of infamy and rather overcompensated in their memorial.

The Cromarty Firth is an excellent anchorage and Invergordon was once an important naval base. HMS *Natal* blew up on New Year's Eve in 1915, probably owing to carelessness but with a residual suspicion of sabotage. Some local people were killed, attending festivities on board ship at the time. Nowadays the only 'ships' at anchor in the Cromarty Firth are the ubiquitous oil-drilling platforms, which are not drilling for black gold but which are redundant, awaiting disposal. The oil-rig construction yard at Nigg always seems to be facing imminent closure, but at least survived into the new millennium. The Invergordon smelter, once heralded as the economic salvation of this part of the northern Highlands, is long gone.

Further north, on what is now called the Dornoch Firth but which on the oldest maps is described as the 'Firth of Tayn', the ancient royal burgh of Tain is certainly worth the short detour off the main road. The church is associated with St Duthac and was an important centre of pilgrimage in the Middle Ages. A small museum and heritage centre beside the church interprets this history.

To the east of Tain another peninsula juts out into the North Sea, ending up at Tarbat Ness. The village of Portmahomack is unusual in being an east-coast town which faces west, with good views of Ben Wyvis (3,432ft; 1,046m) and the mountains of Sutherland. An excellent museum occupies the former church on the edge of the village. It can be interesting to linger on the seafront at Portmahomack to watch air-force jets on their bombing runs over the range at Inver. They swoop in from the backdrop of the mountains, bank steeply, and plunge almost to ground level over their target before climbing off for another run – quite a contrast from the natural magnificence of the scenery.

The so-called 'Seaboard Villages' of Hilton of Cadboll, Balintore and Shandwick, on the east coast of the Tarbat peninsula, are small, traditional fishing villages giving a glimpse of a former way of life. Overlooking Shandwick an important Pictish stone has recently been conserved and a protective shelter erected around it, with some interpretative panels. This highly decorated stone tells a story of hunting and kingship which brings the enigmatic Picts momentarily to life. A visit to this stone, to the Tarbat Heritage Centre at Portmahomack and the Groam House Museum at Rosemarkie on the Black Isle will give the visitor almost as much knowledge of the Picts as we possess.

INVERGORDON NAVAL MUTINY, 1931

In August 1931 there was a national financial crisis which resulted in the collapse of Ramsay MacDonald's Labour government though he continued as Prime Minister in a coalition National Government. An emergency budget raised taxes and reduced the pay of government employees, including naval personnel, some of whom were with HMS Hood *and other vessels in the Cromarty Firth for their autumn naval exercises.*

The first the men knew of their 25 per cent pay cut from 25s to £1 a week was when they read about it in the newspapers in the middle of September. Meetings were held and the men refused to sail, though it was more passive resistance than overt mutiny. Sailors sang the 'Red Flag' and sea shanties, and held more meetings. The Admiral was recalled to London and after a few days word came through that the cuts in pay would be reduced to 22s 6d. One by one the ships sailed back to their home ports and the 'mutiny' crumbled. The autumn exercises were cancelled. In 1933 the largest fleet ever seen in the Cromarty Firth arrived with over 20,000 men and this set the pattern for the remaining years of peace in the period before World War II.

The Eagle Stone in the spa town of Strathpeffer, west of Dingwall, has incised Pictish symbols

Pages 30–1: On the summit of Knock Farrell, near Strathpeffer

2 SUTHERLAND AND CAITHNESS

EAST SUTHERLAND

ONCE WE CROSS THE DORNOCH FIRTH bridge we have crossed a cultural boundary into the old county of Sutherland. Although Norsemen penetrated further south into Easter Ross the Dornoch Firth represents the major natural boundary between the lands of Scotland on the south side, with the royal burgh and pilgrim centre of Tain, and the lands of the Norse to the north, ruled by the Earls of Orkney and ultimately by the Kings of Norway.

Of the 13,000 people who live today in the old county of Sutherland, about 8,500 live in the string of villages along the eastern shore of the county, facing the North Sea: Dornoch, Golspie, Brora and Helmsdale. Though sparsely populated, Sutherland covers a big area – the whole of the north of Scotland north of the Dornoch Firth on the east coast and north of Ullapool on the west coast, except for the small county of Caithness occupying a triangle right up in the north-east corner of Scotland.

Dornoch was the county town of Sutherland, and is the first village reached after crossing the new bridge over the Dornoch Firth. It is still an important administrative centre. Dornoch Cathedral dates from the thirteenth century and is a real architectural gem, though tiny. Across the road is the Bishop's Palace, a sixteenth-century fortified house, much altered. The cathedral contains tombs and memorials of the infamous Sutherland family responsible for some of the worst excesses of the Highland Clearances. On the other hand, the same family provided money and resources to repair and restore the cathedral. Perhaps it was to provide a fitting memorial for a duke, but we can enjoy the result none the less. Dornoch is also world-renowned for its championship links golf course, dating back to 1616. There is a Tourist Information Centre in the town centre.

Andrew Carnegie lived at nearby Skibo Castle, a sprawling mansion now a luxury hotel. The village of Embo, on the coast just north of Dornoch, is of note for being the last enclave of east-coast Sutherland Gaelic, a linguistic pocket of the ancient language once spoken by the entire population. Embo is perhaps more famous today as the site of the original 'Grannie's Heilan' Hame', immortalised in a sentimental ballad.

Above: A gargoyle guarding the roof of Dornoch Cathedral

Opposite: The interior of Dornoch Cathedral, dating from the thirteenth century

THE NORSE

The first Viking raiders attacked Christian monasteries in the Hebrides, including Iona, from AD794, eventually driving the Christian religion underground. Their motives included sacred loot (some of the finest Celtic silverwork is in Scandinavian museums) and the knowledge that the God of the Christian church was a threat to Odin and his entourage. They were also very interested in one of the most lucrative commodities available in the Hebrides – slaves, preferably female, many of whom were resettled in the new Norse colonies in Iceland.

In the Northern Isles and in the Hebrides, local culture was almost completely submerged by Norse settlers, who farmed peacefully for many generations. Norse influence extended first to Caithness on the Scottish mainland and then to Sutherland, eventually reaching Dingwall and the Beauly Firth – a Norse place of assembly was a Thingvollr. *On the west coast, the Norse occupied all the islands and parts of the adjacent mainland, right down to the Isle of Man and Dublin. Norse sovereignty of Scottish territories was transferred to the Kingdom of Scotland by the Treaty of Perth in 1266, though long before that effective control had been lost. Under Somerled (d. 1164) and his MacDonald descendants Gaelic culture was re-established.*

Right & opposite: Dunrobin Castle was extensively remodelled in the mid-nineteenth century

Visiting Dornoch and Embo requires a small detour off the main A9 road, but is certainly worth the effort. The cathedral is a very special piece of Highland history, not to be missed.

Further up the coast is Golspie, which is effectively a 'company town' – on the northern edge of the village is Dunrobin Castle, the historic seat of the Earls and Dukes of Sutherland. It is open to the public, along with its gardens and grounds. The castle looks as if it is left over from a Disney film set, but its core is a thirteenth-century stronghold. Later extensions and additions have transformed the spartan original into a fairy-tale château which would seem less out of place on the Loire.

Throughout the nineteenth century, and well into the twentieth, Dunrobin entertained a glittering array of interesting and titled visitors. One was Harriet Beecher Stowe, the American writer of *Uncle Tom's Cabin*, whose book *Sunny memories of a foreign land* inspired Donald Macleod's *Gloomy memories*, a damning history of the Highland Clearances. Its full title gives a hint of the horrors described in this important book: *Gloomy memories in the Highlands of Scotland versus Harriet Beecher Stowe's Sunny memories in (England) a foreign land: or, a faithful picture of the extirpation of the Celtic race from the Highlands of Scotland.* 'Extirpation' in the nineteenth century conjured up just as terrible images as 'ethnic cleansing' in the twentieth.

Overlooking Golspie is a notorious statue commemorating the first Duke of Sutherland, George Granville Leveson-Gower (1758-1833), Marquess of Stafford after 1803. His wife Elizabeth was Countess of Sutherland in her own right. Along with their agents and servants,

Right: The statue of the first Duke of
Sutherland on Ben a'Bhragaidh, above
Golspie, is easily reached by a well-
maintained track (Author)

*Right: The statue of the first Duke of
Sutherland on Ben a'Bhragaidh, above
Golspie, is easily reached by a well-
maintained track (Author)*

*Opposite: The castle at Girnigoe, just
south of Wick in Caithness, was built by
William Sinclair, 2nd Earl of Caithness,
after he had surrendered his earldom of
Orkney to the crown in 1472; it was
destroyed in 1690*

especially the hated Patrick Sellar, the factor (estate manager) for the
Sutherland estates, they were among the most despised individuals in the
Highlands – outside of Golspie. The debate continues as to whether the
statue on Beinn a'Bhragaidh should be retained as a symbol of ruthless
oppression and cultural genocide, or demolished as an obscene reminder of
a sad period in Highland history. 'The Mannie', as he is called locally, stands
with his back to the real monuments to the Highland Clearances – the
empty glens and roofless ruins scattered throughout the whole of the
Highlands and Islands.

Continuing up the east-coast road we reach the village of Brora, where
two major industries have closed in recent years. The coal mine was a
victim of economic forces, while the military communications centre
closed as part of the 'peace dividend' at the end of the Cold War. A woollen
mill and textile factory in the town survives, precariously.

Right on the northern edge of Sutherland, just at the border with
Caithness, is the village of Helmsdale. Here is the award-winning Timespan
heritage centre, where the story of the Clearances is told. The old name for
the river which reaches the sea at Helmsdale (a Norse place-name) is the
Ullie – a very ancient name which is recorded by Ptolemy in the first
century AD. It is one of the great salmon-fishing rivers of the Highlands.
Inland it flows through the Strath of Kildonan, where the population was
reduced from 1,574 in 1811 to a mere 257 by 1831, in the most fearful of
the Sutherland Clearances initiated by the Countess of Sutherland and her
hated factor, Patrick Sellar. Some of the tenants evicted from Kildonan
found their way across the Atlantic, but most were resettled in the coastal
villages of Caithness and Sutherland. Ironically, later in the nineteenth
century, Kildonan was briefly the centre of a small-scale gold rush, after
gold was found in the Helmsdale River.

CAITHNESS

The county of Caithness could hardly be described as part of the northern Highlands, yet it seems churlish to omit it from this book. Once you are 'Over the Ord' (the hill at the southern boundary) you are in a different world, in a culture more Norse than Scots – reflected in the local speech and accent. Even the geology is different: Caithness is flagstone country, from where come many of the paving slabs for our great cities. They are used instead of drystone dykes for field boundaries – thin slabs of flagstone (actually a type of slate) placed vertically in the ground.

This is an area fiercely proud of its history and identity, which guards its distinctiveness jealously – and yet, it is not locked into some mythical past but very much in the forefront of atomic technology, through the nuclear facility and reprocessing plant at Dounreay. The population of Caithness is about 25,000, most of whom live in the two towns of Wick and Thurso. Wick was the former county town of Caithness and has about 8,500 residents, while Thurso is slightly bigger with a population of about 9,000. There is naturally great rivalry between the two places. Wick certainly dates back to Viking times, as its name means 'bay' in Norse. It was a royal burgh in the Middle Ages. Pulteneytown, now considered part of Wick, except by the people who live there, gets its name from the patron of Thomas Telford, who was commissioned in the early 1800s to create a new harbour there. Wick was the herring capital of Europe in 1817, when 60,000 barrels were exported, but it suffered with the decline of that industry and is still an unemployment blackspot. The world-famous Caithness Glass factory is one success story in an otherwise depressed economy. There is a Tourist Information Centre in Wick and an interesting local heritage centre at the old harbour.

DOUNREAY

Beside the ruins of a medieval castle, is the tell-tale sphere of Dounreay's nuclear reactor. The fast-breeder reactor programme has now come to an end, but the controversial decision to get involved in reprocessing other people's nuclear fuel has guaranteed its continued existence. Even 'decommissioning' existing facilities will take many decades and billions of pounds. Situated for safety reasons as far as possible from metropolitan London, suspicions of a link between Dounreay and a 'leukemia cluster' in Caithness have never been proved, but doubts remain. Radioactive particles are routinely found on the sandy seashore nearby, and when archaeologists were asked to examine the castle ruins they had to take safety precautions and go through full decontamination procedures. It is now evident that the reactor was built too close to the shoreline, as coastal erosion is threatening to undermine waste-storage shafts in the next few decades.

Above: The nuclear research facility at Dounreay, on the north coast

Left: Caithness Glass factory interior

Opposite: Sea stacks off the coast of Caithness

Pages 40–1: The Stacks of Duncansby, near John o'Groats and the Duncansby Head lighthouse, looking across the Pentland Firth to the island of Stroma and Orkney

Above: The lighthouse on Dunnet Head, the most northerly point of the Scottish mainland, looking across the Pentland Firth to the islands of Orkney

Opposite above & below: The Grey Cairns of Camster, inland from Lybster, are communal burial monuments built from local flagstone during the Neolithic period, dating from before 2500BC

Thurso is only 20 miles (32km) away but has a totally different 'feel' to it. The town blossomed in the last half of the twentieth century, largely due to the nearby Dounreay nuclear-reactor research facility, started in 1954, and which is open to the public.

Sir John Sinclair of Ulbster (1754-1835) was born in Thurso Castle, on the outskirts of the town. He was a noted agricultural reformer and edited the *Statistical Account of Scotland* in the 1790s. This is a parish-by-parish history and description of Scotland as it was at the end of the eighteenth century and is still used by historians as an unrivalled source of information on social conditions, population statistics, and historical details. Thurso was also the birthplace of Sir William Smith (1854-1914), the founder of the Boys' Brigade.

Both Wick and Thurso are connected to Inverness by rail. There is an airport at Wick and a ferry service from Scrabster (near Thurso) to Orkney, with seasonal connections to Shetland.

East of Thurso is Dunnet Head, the most northerly point of the mainland of Britain, a promontory with magnificent cliff scenery on which perches a lighthouse. The parish of Dunnet is memorable for one of its incumbents, the cartographer Timothy Pont, who single-handedly carried out the mapping of Scotland in manuscript between 1585 and 1595. He died without seeing his project realised, but fifty years later the Amsterdam mapmaker Blaeu published the edited manuscripts as beautifully engraved maps in a magnificent atlas. Some of Pont's manuscript maps survive in the

National Library of Scotland. They are important sources in the study of Scottish local history.

East of Dunnet Head is John o'Groats, which is about 870 miles (1,400km) from Land's End, in Cornwall. Sir John Sinclair tells the story in his *Statistical Account* of how the Dutchman Jan de Grot came to Caithness in the reign of James IV and built an octagonal house for his eight sons. The ferry service which he operated to the Orkney island of South Ronaldsay, just over 6 miles (9.6km) across the choppy waters of the Pentland Firth, still exists today in modified form. Tourists can have their photographs taken at John o'Groats in front of a signpost indicating the mileage to their home town.

Between Dunnet Head and John o'Groats is the Castle of Mey, formerly Barrogill Castle, for many years the property of Her Majesty Queen Elizabeth, the Queen Mother. The core of the castle dates from 1606.

Dunbeath, one of the herring-fishery villages on the east coast of Caithness, was the birthplace of the novelist Neil Gunn (1891-1973) and is described in his writings, such as *The Grey Coast, Morning Tide, Highland River* and *The Silver Darlings*. His novels are all back in print and their great importance recognised, after decades of neglect. Highland life is chronicled movingly and memorably in Gunn's works, especially in *Highland River*, where the course of his native river to the sea is taken as a metaphor for his own growth and development.

Two of the most interesting and best-preserved archaeological sites in the Highlands are in Caithness, near the village of Lybster. The Neolithic Grey Cairns of Camster, over 5,800 years old, were communal burial places, built with great community effort and great skill. They have been excavated and sympathetically restored. Also near Lybster, at Mid Clyth, are enigmatic stone rows, probably dating from the Bronze Age, around 1500BC.

Standing stones and stone circles are commonplace throughout Scotland and particularly in the north-west Highlands, but stone rows are unusual and it has been suggested that they may represent a kind of mathematical grid on which complex astronomical calculations were worked out, relating to the orbit of the moon and hence linked to eclipse prediction. The only comparable sites are in Cornwall and Brittany, at the opposite end of a Bronze Age cultural province.

NORTH-WEST SUTHERLAND

The north-west corner of Scotland, part of the old county of Sutherland, is surely the wildest and remotest corner of Britain and one of the last 'wildernesses' in Europe. Outside of the short summer season you can drive for miles and miles and miles and never meet another car. You may however meet enormous articulated lorries carrying catches from the fishing ports of Lochinver and Kinlochbervie, or delivery trucks bringing essential goods from depots in Inverness, or mobile libraries bringing books to the remotest doorsteps, or the occasional bus taking children to and from school, or shoppers to the supermarkets and shopping emporia of Inverness.

In the summer, things can be very different. In June, July and August the cars you see are likely to have foreign licence plates, from Germany, France, Italy, Spain and Switzerland. Or, dare we say, from England! If it's a camper van, it's usually Italian; if it's a car towing a caravan – barely suitable on single-track roads – it's usually English holidaymakers. The roads are quite a contrast from the fast, improved A9 on the east coast. Single-track roads are a revelation to the unwary, and have an etiquette all of their own. Passing places, marked by striped black-and-white poles, are frequent, but the skill in knowing when to stop and when to risk making a dash for the next one, when you can see a vehicle approaching, is a skill that has to be learned. It helps if you know the road! To the locals it comes naturally, but visitors can often get it horribly wrong.

Perhaps the best way to approach north-west Sutherland is through the gateway village of Lairg. Lairg is apparently in the middle of nowhere, but it has a railway station and an important auction mart to which farmers bring their sheep and cattle for the sales. To reach Lairg, turn off the main A9 east-coast road either just before or just after crossing the Dornoch Firth bridge, through Bonar Bridge – which has a bridge, a modern 'stone circle' of boulders representing the different geology of the area, but not much else. Up on the hill above Bonar Bridge is the Migdale cottage hospital, the core of which was a poorhouse in the nineteenth century.

Lairg is at the southern end of Loch Shin, a photogenic stretch of water 17 miles (27km) long, with a dam and hydro-electric station. After leaving Loch Shin it is another 20 miles (32km) to the road junction at Laxford Bridge, through truly stunning scenery. One thing the visitor learns quickly in Sutherland is that it takes much longer to drive anywhere than you would expect – the 37 miles (60km) from Lairg to Laxford Bridge will certainly take nearly an hour. Longer, of course, if you are seduced by the many tempting views which deserve to be enjoyed and perhaps photographed at an even more leisurely pace.

From the junction at Laxford Bridge it is another 7 miles (11km) to Scourie. A sheltered bay, sandy beaches, wonderful sunsets and

Above: Strathy Point lighthouse, on the north coast of Sutherland

Opposite: Stone rows at Mid-Clyth, just north of Lybster in Caithness, date from the Bronze Age and are paralleled by similar arrangements on Dartmoor and at Carnac, in Brittany

THE ETIQUETTE OF NARROW ROADS

A crucial piece of courteous behaviour which some visitors seem to ignore is that if you are being followed closely by another car, you should pull into a passing place and allow it to pass. This goes against the grain for southern commuters who are used to defending their space at all costs, but the car behind could be the local doctor on his way to an emergency call, somebody heading to Inverness for a medical appointment, or just a frustrated local who knows the road well and doesn't want to dawdle along admiring the scenery.

Pages 46–7: Coastal scenery east of Durness

Above: The Falls of Shin, on the road between Bonar Bridge and Lairg

surrounding mountainous scenery make this a perfect place to relax and enjoy the beauties of nature – but the same could be said of countless other small communities up and down the west coast.

From Scourie there is a choice of heading south to Kylestrome, but having come this far it would be a shame not to aim for the north coast, and Durness. So, returning to Laxford Bridge, we head north with the peaks of Foinaven (2,989ft; 911m) and Arkle (2,583ft; 787m) inland, until we reach Rhiconich. The detour to the modern fishing port of Kinlochbervie and the quaintly named Oldshoremore is worthwhile – but allow plenty of time on these twisty roads. North from Oldshoremore is Sandwood Bay, reached only on foot, but a popular destination for those in the know for its unspoiled environment and miles of sandy beaches.

From Rhiconich it is 14 miles (23km) to Durness, on the north coast of Sutherland, which is the closest most people will get to Cape Wrath, the north-west tip of Scotland. Near Durness is the craft village of Balnakeil, on the site of an old army camp, now something of a haven for those who enjoy an alternative life style. Some extremely talented artists, potters and other craftspeople may tempt the visitor with their wares. Two miles (3.2km) east of Durness the Smoo Cave has been a tourist attraction since Sir Walter Scott's visit in 1814. The large limestone cave is decorated with stalactites and stalagmites.

From Durness the road east follows the twists and turns of the north coast around Loch Eriboll past the Melness road end to the village of Tongue – 38 miles (61km) in all. Along the north coast, in Mackay country, a series of lochs aligned on a north-south axis point like fingers deep into the Sutherland hinterland: the Kyle of Durness, Loch Eriboll, Loch Hope and the Kyle of Tongue. A 'kyle' is a fjord-like sound of water, from the Gaelic *caol*. The north-west of Sutherland is the district of Eddrachilis, meaning 'between the kyles' in Gaelic. The original spelling is *eadar a' chaoilais*. To the south the mountains of Ben Hope (3,041ft; 927m) and Ben Loyal (2,507ft; 764m) are prominent. The views of Ben Loyal are especially good. From Tongue the road continues east, eventually reaching Thurso in Caithness after some 44 miles (71km). The village of Bettyhill is 13 miles (21km) from Tongue, on the coast where Strath Naver meets the sea. This valley was the scene of some of the worst excesses of the Sutherland Clearances. It was here, between 1814 and 1819, that Patrick Sellar cleared off all the tenants to make way for more profitable flocks of sheep – and a few shepherds. In 1816 Sellar stood trial in Inverness for the atrocities committed in his name, but was acquitted. The village of Bettyhill is named after Elizabeth, Countess of Sutherland, the wife of the Duke of Sutherland. There is a small heritage centre in Bettyhill, in the former Farr parish church, which has an important ninth-century Pictish cross in the graveyard. Farr Secondary School educates scholars from a wide hinterland.

From Tongue a road runs due south, below Ben Loyal and along the west shore of Loch Loyal, to Altnaharra and eventually, after 37 miles (60km) back to Lairg. The round trip from Lairg to Laxford Bridge, Scourie, Rhiconich, Kinlochbervie, Durness, Tongue and Bettyhill would make an excellent day out – in suitable weather!

Smoo Cave, near Durness, north-west Sutherland

Page 50–1: Sandy beach at Sango Bay near Durness

CROFTING

In the Highlands a 'croft' is described as 'a piece of land surrounded by regulations'. Being strictly accurate a croft is not a house but the land upon which it stands, though in popular usage this distinction has become blurred.

More surprisingly, crofting is a system of land-holding which is in no way traditional to the Highland way of life, but which arose early in the nineteenth century and quickly gained currency after the reorganisation of Highland agriculture accelerated. The traditional kind of landholding in the Highlands was communal; a township would divide up their arable and grazing land equitably and organise agricultural work collectively on an agreed rota.

Part of the process of the Highland Clearances was the removal of farming communities to infertile coastal locations, where tenants were located to 'crofts' and charged economic rents. The many abuses suffered by Highland tenant farmers eventually led to a period of radical agitation as a result of which Gladstone's government supported a parliamentary bill which eventually became the Crofters' Holdings Act of 1886. Subsequent legislation strengthened crofters' rights and in 1955 a Crofters' Commission was established and in more recent times a Crofters' Union. There are about 18,000 crofts throughout the Highlands and Islands consisting of an average of 4 acres (1.6 ha) of arable land with access to communal grazing land nearby.

ASSYNT

South from Scourie, at Kylestrome, a dramatic new concrete bridge carries the road across the narrows of Kylesku into the district of Assynt. The landscape is dominated by the distinctive mountains of Assynt: Canisp, Suilven, Stac Pollaidh, Quinag and Ben More Assynt. The very names conjure up an image of these sculpted buttresses of Torridonian sandstone on a gneiss base, mountainous pillars soaring out of the surrounding moors and lochans.

The geology of north-west Sutherland is very complex and attracts students and interested amateur rockhounds from all over Britain and indeed from all over the world, for in the early history of the science of geology this was one of the areas where the story of the rocks was first worked out. From Lochinver all the way north to Cape Wrath there is a coastal strip of Lewisian gneiss, 10 miles (16km) wide, with gneiss and Torridonian patches north of Scourie.

This ancient rock is also found in the Hebrides (especially on the island of Lewis from where it takes its name) but it is also found on the other side of the Atlantic, in Greenland and Newfoundland, showing that at one time there was an enormous continental landmass where the Atlantic Ocean is now. The mid-Atlantic ridge, on the ocean floor, shows where the continent has been split and torn apart, leaving what once were neighbouring rocks now thousands of miles apart.

Assynt has entered the modern folklore of the Highlands through the exploits of the Assynt crofters, local small-scale farmers and fishermen who banded together to purchase the North Lochinver Estate when it came on the market in June 1992. After many adventures the buy-out was successfully completed in December 1992 and in February 1993 the Assynt Crofters' Trust took possession of 21,300 acres (9,000ha) of land, with thirteen townships. Land ownership and land reform is today a big issue everywhere in the Highlands, but it was the Assynt crofters who led the way and blazed the trail of community ownership now followed by the people of Knoydart, the islanders of Eigg and by a long queue of like-minded estate tenants all over the Highlands. The Assynt crofters proved that native Highlanders can own their own land, administer it effectively and run it profitably.

The fishing ports of Kinlochbervie and Lochinver have benefited from the investment of millions of pounds in new piers and storage facilities, essential to the survival of the local fishing fleets. Much of the investment is the result of the region's qualification for 'Objective 1' structural funding from the European Union.

The road from Inchnadamph to Lochinver, alongside Loch Assynt, nearly 7 miles (11km) long, and beside the mountains of Quinag (2,651ft; 808m) and Glasven (2,546ft; 776m) is one of the loveliest in Scotland. The views

THE GEOLOGY OF ASSYNT

In Assynt, between Lochinver and Scourie, the geology is almost entirely composed of gneiss, with its typical 'knob and lochan' landscape. Gneiss is an extremely hard rock, typically with pink and grey swirls. It looks at its best after a shower of rain – not unusual in these parts! A pebble of gneiss from the beach, an example of the oldest rock in Europe, perhaps more than half the age of the earth itself, would make an evocative memory of north-west Scotland for the visitor's mantlepiece.

Page 53: Lighthouse on the Point of Stoer, north of Lochinver

Above: Ardvreck Castle, in Assynt, is a late-fifteenth century Macleod stronghold where James Graham, the Marquis of Montrose, was captured in 1650, ending the civil wars in Scotland

grace many pictorial calendars and postcards. Ardvreck Castle on Loch Assynt is where the royalist commander Montrose was betrayed in 1650.

South of Lochinver the single-track road twists its way through a tortured landscape, rejoining the main road north of Ullapool. There is an excellent bookshop and tea room with local crafts and souvenirs at Inverkirkaig. Between this junction and Inchnadamph another road leads off to the east through Strath Oykell to Lairg and Bonar Bridge.

The poet Norman MacCaig, writing in English but of Assynt stock, described the lands of north-west Sutherland beautifully in many of his poems. One of his more whimsical poems encapsulates one of the topical issues in the Highlands today:

'Characteristics'

My American friends
who claim Scottish ancestry,
have been touring Scotland.
In ten days they visited
eleven castles. I smiled -
How American.
They said they preferred
the ruined ones. I smiled again.
How Scottish.

THE CLEARANCES

Before leaving Sutherland we will pause for a moment to reflect on the period of the Highland Clearances, the years of famine, the emigrations, and the effect of it all on Gaelic culture and the social and economic history of the Highlands.

Modern Highland history really begins with the disaster of the Battle of Culloden in April 1746. The estates of those chiefs who supported Bonnie Prince Charlie's Jacobite rebellion were forfeited, to be administered by a committee on behalf of the Crown until, a generation or more later, the heir or successors of those chiefs were thought sufficiently reliable to reassume control. In the aftermath of Culloden even the traditional dress of the Highlander was outlawed. The only way for a Highlander to wear the kilt was for him to enlist in the British army – an escape route from poverty, misery and Hanoverian military occupation which was followed by many thousands of men. In 1759 Highlanders of the British army stormed the Heights of Abraham to capture Quebec for General Wolfe and laid siege to the fortress of Louisburg on Cape Breton Island, which after the peace of 1763 became part of British Canada.

The 78th Fraser Highlanders lost 200 men at Quebec; their commander James Wolfe, himself killed there, had been at Culloden in a staff post as a nineteen-year-old Brigade-Major and had been an area commander in the Highlands in the 1750s during the military occupation after Culloden. The irony that some of the men he had faced across the battlefield of Culloden helped him win his own final victory is rather minimised when we know that of his Highland troops at Quebec he wrote that they were:

> ... hardy, intrepid, accustom'd to a rough country, and no great mischief if they fall. How can you better employ a secret enemy than by making his end conducive to the public good.

After the Treaty of Paris in 1763 ceded all French possessions in Canada to King George III, 200 Highlanders took up the offer of land grants and elected to stay behind. Another of the many ironies of Highland history is revealed when we discover that the French settlers of Nova Scotia and Cape Breton were cleared just as ruthlessly by Highland soldiers who had served in the British army as their descendants in Sutherland only fifty years later. Highland soldiers fought for King George against the American colonists in the Revolutionary War. They defended the British Isles against the threat of revolutionary France and helped defeat Napoleon at Waterloo.

After each of these conflicts ended, and with the services of so many soldiers no longer required, some men elected to take their chances in the New World and spurned the opportunity to return home to Highland poverty. Meanwhile, back home, Highland landowners were facing up to

SHEEP IN THE HIGHLANDS

Sheep have been reared in the Highlands from the time of the Neolithic first farmers, over 4,500 years ago. The native breeds were small, dark-woolled and hardy, ideally suited to small-scale subsistence farming. However, the vast flocks of Cheviot sheep which were brought into the Highlands from the Borders – where they had made fortunes for both shepherds and landowners – in the late eighteenth and early nineteenth centuries were very different. Named after the Cheviot Hills on the borders between Scotland and England, where they had been known since the late Middle Ages, the Cheviot breed proved ideally suited to the Highlands. They are larger than the little native breeds, do well in bleak, windswept conditions, are strong and hardy, and require minimal husbandry. They lamb easily and have a strong mothering instinct, and they mature quickly. Their wool has a distinctive resilience and bouncy springiness which is well suited to domestic uses and is often blended into other yarns to give extra resilience and durability.

Page 56–7: The view from Rhu Mor to (left to right) Cul Mor, Stac Pollaidh and Cul Beag (John Cleare)

the problems of running vast estates, often burdened by debt. They preferred to be seen in Edinburgh and London society, with all the expense that entailed. As improvements in agriculture percolated through the land it became clear that the economics of the Highland estate did not make sense to an era which produced Adam Smith and the new ideology of capitalism. First the countryside of England was reorganised and enclosed, with devastating social effects. In Scotland, vast stretches of the Borders were cleared of people and replaced by sheep, but the forgotten 'Lowland Clearances', though disruptive to individuals and families, were seen as ultimately an improvement to the social order. The proximity of Glasgow and Edinburgh in a period when their industrial, manufacturing and productive base was expanding rapidly was a factor which cushioned the traumatic effects of the Lowland Clearances.

It therefore seemed logical, rational, natural and socially beneficial for Highland landlords to apply the same agricultural and economic principles to the Highlands. And so, throughout the Highlands and Islands, starting in the 1780s and 1790s, people were replaced by sheep flocks.

However, the ways in which the new sheep were introduced into the Highlands and the impoverished human inhabitants cleared out to make room varied tremendously from one area to another. Sometimes this was a reflection of local conditions – some estates were in a far worse condition than others – but sometimes it was a matter of the personalities of the main players. The factor of the Sutherland estates, Patrick Sellar, was a cold, ruthlessly single-minded improver, but elsewhere many felt that sheepfarms were inevitable, but did their best to mitigate the worst effects of the social dislocation which ensued.

One of the obvious solutions to the perennial 'Highland problem' was emigration.

One of the most popular destinations for Highland emigrants was Canada, particularly the island of Cape Breton, now part of the province of Nova Scotia. The process of emigration to Nova Scotia is comparatively well documented, largely due to the efforts of Canadian historians. The voyage of the *Hector* from Loch Broom to Pictou, Nova Scotia, in 1773 has been well researched. If the oft-quoted figure of 25 million people in North America of Scottish descent seems excessive, consider that it is reckoned that there are 40,000 people today in Canada and the United States descended from the 200 Highland emigrants on the *Hector*.

The emigrations to Cape Breton peaked in the years around 1830, and between 1827 and 1832 it was probably the principal North American destination for Highland emigrants. Customs House records in Cape Breton document the arrival of 7,300 Scots in those five years, but we know that many more went unrecorded, landed on the deserted west coast of Cape Breton Island. Between 1825 and 1845 at least 12,000 Scots went to Cape Breton, and in the decade from 1815 to 1825 another 9,000 Scots arrived in Nova Scotia, of which at least 2,000 settled in Cape Breton.

MOVEMENT OF A PEOPLE

Perhaps a million people emigrated to North America from the British Isles in the first half of the nineteenth century and perhaps 200,000 of these were Scots, mostly from the Highlands. This figure does not include many more thousands who migrated internally within the United Kingdom, especially to other parts of Scotland. By 1900 it is likely that 500,000 Scots had emigrated overseas, mainly to the USA, Canada, Australia, New Zealand and South Africa and today there can hardly be a country in the world where the two great Scottish festivals of Hogmanay (New Year's Eve) and Burns Night (25 January) are not celebrated with enthusiasm by the Scottish diaspora.

Opposite: Maiden Loch near Clachtoll, north of Lochinver

Pages 60–1: Looking across Clar Loch Mor to Cul Beag and Cul Mor, north of Ullapool

As early as 1802-3, 7,000 Highlanders emigrated to British North America, and another 2,500 in the years up to the American War of 1812. Adding up all these figures, at least 20,000 Scots, most of them Highlanders, had settled in Cape Breton by 1845, when the entire population of the island was 55,000. Most of these Highlanders came from Lochaber and the southern half of the Western Isles: from Arisaig and Moidart, the Small Isles (Rum, Eigg, Muck and Canna), Skye, Barra and the Uists. Most of them were Catholic Highlanders.

In 1931, of 75,000 Nova Scotians of Scottish descent, 24,000 spoke Gaelic. By 1941 this had dropped to 14,000 and by 1991 to less than 1,000, most of them in Cape Breton.

Speak to Highlanders today about emigration to Cape Breton and the chances are, especially if they are from Wester Ross or Assynt, that they will mention the name of the Rev Norman Macleod. It was from near Clachtoll, north of Lochinver, that this determined and rather opinionated young man left his native land. It is difficult to summarise a long and complicated life in just a few words: in an era when religious contentiousness was normal he found it impossible to accept establishment views, and in 1817 he led a group of 400 like-minded people into exile, boarding the barque Frances Ann in Loch Broom, bound for Pictou, Nova Scotia.

In the context of the emigration of 20,000 Catholic Highlanders to Cape Breton, Norman Macleod's odyssey was numerically insignificant, but it is he who has a memorial cairn on the beach at Clachtoll, not the 20,000. He was a restless spirit, unhappy and intolerant in the company of people who did not share his views. He lasted three years in Pictou then led his people over to Cape Breton, to the settlement of St Ann's. They stayed there for thirty years, until Cape Breton also became too crowded, and in 1851 he began a complicated logistical process which eventually resulted in six ships transporting 800 of his followers to the other side of the world, first to Australia and then to New Zealand, where they settled at Waipu, north of Auckland, in the 1850s. Norman Macleod died there in 1866, but many descendants of his group remain.

3 WESTER ROSS, APPLECROSS AND LOCHALSH

WESTER ROSS AND TORRIDON

THEY ALWAYS SAY IN THE HIGHLANDS that 'the best is in the west', and if it's dramatic scenery and mountain grandeur you are after, there is no doubt that the western side of the county of Ross and Cromarty takes some beating. This is 'Wester Ross', so named to distinguish it from 'Easter Ross' on the east side of the county, facing the North Sea. Wester Ross is a land of towering, sculpted mountain peaks, especially in the area of Torridon. By contrast, it is also a land of sea lochs winding deep into the mountainous heartland. This combination of sea and mountain enhances the grandeur of the scenery.

Driving westwards from Dingwall across the main cross-country route to Wester Ross, the road skirts the lumpish mass of Ben Wyvis (3,432ft; 1,046m) and passes through the old spa town of Strathpeffer, where wealthy visitors once came annually to 'take the waters' and get their names listed in the 'society' columns of the local newspaper. Many of the Victorian buildings in Strathpeffer have been restored and renovated in recent years, and the Pump Room is back in working use. In its heyday, before World War I, the sulphur and chalybeate waters were held to be beneficial for rheumatic conditions, gout, skin problems and liver troubles. There is a Museum of Childhood in the village.

Near Strathpeffer is the 'Eagle Stone' – a Pictish symbol stone – and Knockfarrel vitrified fort, one of the finest anywhere, with magnificent views from the summit. The panorama includes the whole bulk of Ben Wyvis, the peaks around Strathconan, the waters of the Cromarty Firth and the pass through to Garve and the west. Nearer at hand is the estate of Brahan, associated with Coinneach (Kenneth) Odhar – the 'Brahan Seer' (see page 24).

The road to Ullapool passes through wild, empty lands. At Garve, 13 miles (21km) from Dingwall the road divides; the

The fishing village and ferry terminal of Ullapool

The Views fron Ben Wyvis

*The ascent of Ben Wyvis (3,432ft;
1,046m) from the Ullapool road is
lengthy but straightforward. This is
a rather dull mountain compared
with the breathtaking excitement of
Torridon, but the views from the top
are superb – the coast of the Moray
Firth from Inverness to Lossiemouth,
the Cairngorms from Ben Macdui to
Ben Rinnes, and northwards to the
Ord of Caithness and Morven.*

*Above: Looking up Loch Broom from
Ullapool*

*Opposite: Corrieshalloch Gorge and the
Falls of Measach, on the road between
Garve and Ullapool*

northern branch heads north-west to Ullapool while the southern branch
heads for Achnasheen, Strathcarron and Applecross.

Ullapool is built on a promontory jutting out into Loch Broom and was
established there by the British Fisheries Society in 1788. This is the major
mainland ferry terminal for the Western Isles, with daily sailings to
Stornoway on the Isle of Lewis. Ullapool is the largest village in Wester
Ross, with a population of just over one thousand. Its founders hoped to
take advantage of the herring fishery, but even by 1830 it was clear that
herring stocks were in decline and the village never fulfilled its early
promise. There is an excellent local museum in a former church. A new
secondary-school complex, incorporating the public library and a
community centre, has greatly enhanced Ullapool's facilities.

Despite its isolation, Ullapool has acquired something of a reputation as
an outpost of cultural and literary pursuits, due in large part to the
innovative and creative interest of the owners of the Ceilidh Place, a local
hostelry, restaurant and bookshop. During the long northern winters
poetry readings and art exhibitions brighten up the local scene and at any
time of the year there is good music to be enjoyed somewhere in Ullapool.

Across Loch Broom, at Altnaharrie, is one of Scotland's most famous
restaurants, reached only by a small passenger-ferry service from Ullapool.
Diners are required to stay overnight. Also on the isolated west shore of

In the later Iron Age, well after the period of hilltop hill forts, a variety of smaller, family-sized defensive structures were constructed throughout the Highlands and Islands. Small drystone forts, essentially defended farmsteads, are known as duns *(from the Gaelic word for 'fort'); there are hundreds of examples in the Highlands, mainly in coastal locations, usually on craggy outcrops or headlands. Usually a dun has one thick stone wall, with an entrance passage defended by guard cells and door bars. These structures were open to the elements, but lean-to constructions were built against the inside wall.*

Brochs were tall, circular stone towers, unique to Scotland. About 500 examples have been identified, of which the vast majority are in the Northern Isles, the Hebrides, and Caithness, and the northern and western coasts of the Highlands. Most stood 32–48ft (10–15m) tall and have the distinctive construction feature of a 'hollow wall', without which they would have collapsed under their own weight. Within the walls galleries and staircases were constructed, allowing access to the wallhead. Most have a central hearth and some have a 'scarcement ledge' on which a floor may have rested, allowing the space underneath to be used for storage and animals. Within the Highlands the finest examples are in Glenelg. They date from 100BC and AD100. On older maps they are sometimes referred to as 'Pictish towers'.

Loch Broom, at Rhiroy, is an important Iron Age broch, and the important site of Dun Lagaidh, a multi-period fortified site with a vitrified fort, late Iron Age dun or broch and also medieval remains.

Adventurous visitors to Ullapool may consider expanding their horizons by way of the Caledonian MacBrayne car ferry across the Minch to Stornoway, a journey of just over two-and-a-half hours – in good weather. 'Island-hopping' is one of Calmac's best marketing ideas, with attractive packages available. Once in Stornoway, on Lewis, it is possible to travel south by road to Tarbert, the ferry port of Harris. From there a 'triangular' ferry service links Uig on the Isle of Skye to Lochmaddy in North Uist. Causeways now link North Uist to the islands of Benbecula and South Uist, from where another ferry connects to Barra. A further causeway joins up the island of Vatersay to the road system of the Western Isles. Many variations of this itinerary are possible, perhaps connecting with Calmac's ferries from South Uist and Barra to Oban, in Argyll. From there, similar island-hopping expeditions are possible in the southern isles to destinations such as Lismore, Mull, Coll, Tiree, Colonsay, Islay, Jura, Gigha, Kintyre, Arran and Bute – island-bagging has never been so easy!

North of Ullapool, on the fringes of the spectacular mountains of Sutherland, a road turns west for Achiltibuie, an isolated part of Wester Ross famous for its 'hydroponicum' and its views of the Summer Isles, at

TORRIDON'S MAGNETIC APPEAL

It is not just climbers and hill-walkers who are drawn to Torridon by the magnetism of its mountains. Geologists come to admire their structure: the red Torridonian sandstone which makes up the bulk of Liathach and Beinn Eighe is reckoned as being 750 million years old, while the white quartzite of their summit ridges is a mere 600 million years of age. Access to these mountains is straightforward, but for this reason they often prove more lethal than more remote peaks, and deserve respect at any season of the year, but especially in winter.

the entrance to Loch Broom. The largest of these little islands, Tanera Mor, was farmed by Sir Frank Fraser Darling during the years of World War II. Here Scotland's most famous naturalist successfully cultivated land which was once home to over 100 people, but by the 1930s was abandoned and deserted. His experiences, chronicled in his book *Island Farm*, gave him the confidence and impetus to undertake his *West Highland Survey*, perhaps the most important piece of research into what he described as the 'human ecology' of the Highlands. It should be required reading for today's social engineers.

South of Ullapool the landscape is just as varied and interesting and the scenery if anything even more spectacular than the mountains of Assynt. It is an exciting drive of 24 miles (39km) from Ullapool to Gairloch, a village and fishing port with a Tourist Information Centre and a fine little heritage museum. The sandy shores around Loch Gairloch provide good bathing and fishing. The islands in the sea loch and the views to the south and south-west give this little village one of the loveliest settings in the Scottish Highlands. Away to the south-west, across the Inner Sound, there are distant views of the Cuillins in Skye, while to the south the view is of the mountains of the Flowerdale Forest and Shieldaig Forest, with beyond them Beinn Alligin (3,235ft; 986m) and the mountains of Torridon.

The road from Ullapool to Gairloch winds around the coast past Little Loch Broom to Gruinard Bay and Aultbea. Gruinard Island was used during World War II for experiments with anthrax bombs and has only recently been decontaminated and declared safe. Loch Ewe was an important centre of naval operations during the war and was used for assembling convoys. Aultbea became a major NATO supply base. In Loch Ewe, off Aultbea, is the Isle of Ewe; don't forget to point it out to somebody you care about, preferably by repeating the name of the island several times in quick succession – try it!

From Gairloch a narrow but highly scenic road runs north through North Erradale towards Melvaig, beyond which is the lonely Rudha Reidh, with a lighthouse. South of Gairloch another spur of road leads to the crofting townships of Badachro, Opinan and South Erradale. The main A832 road runs inland from Gairloch to Loch Maree, one of the most beautiful of Scotland's lochs, named after Maelrubha, an early Celtic saint. Slioch (3,215ft; 980m), the photogenic mountain on the east side of Loch Maree, is best viewed from this road. The Loch Maree Hotel was associated with a food-poisoning tragedy in 1922 when six visitors and two 'ghillies' died after eating wild-duck paste sandwiches while fishing on the loch. The incident caused a sensation at the time – 'all the more regrettable,' said the *Inverness Courier*, 'seeing it has occurred at the height of the holiday season'. The potted meat was manufactured by 'one of the best-known brands on the market' (Lazenby's & Sons Ltd). No blame was attached to the hotel. The medical report identified the toxin *bacillus botulinus* as the cause of death. The hotel was well known throughout the Highlands and had been

visited by Queen Victoria in 1877. The Fatal Accident Enquiry into the deaths recommended that a code be added to all processed-food containers and packaging so that the 'trail' of the ingredients could be followed, if necessary.

At the south end of Loch Maree is the village of Kinlochewe. There were once iron mines in this locality, and iron-smelting, linked to charcoal production from the wooded mountain slopes all around – wooded, at least, before the introduction of sheep in the early nineteenth century denuded much of the landscape of its native flora.

At Kinlochewe the main road continues east to Achnasheen and eventually to Dingwall on the east coast, but any visit to Wester Ross would be incomplete without an excursion through the mountain fastness of Torridon to the wilds of Applecross.

The mountains of Torridon dominate this landscape – Old Red Sandstone sculpted into spectacular shapes by glaciers, capped with hard, resistant quartzite. In the final moments of a west-coast sunset, the red bands of sandstone and the white quartzite summits gleam in vibrant colours. The effect can be quite remarkable, though often fleeting.

Beinn Eighe (3,314ft; 972m) and Liathach (3,458ft; 1,054m) are the most dramatic peaks, with Beinn Alligin (3,235ft; 986m) and Beinn Dearg (2,999ft; 914m) to the west and north. The Torridon Estate has been run by the NTS since 1967; with the addition of an area to the west of the main estate it now controls over 16,000 acres (6,475ha) of unsurpassed mountain scenery between Loch Torridon to the south and Loch Maree to the north. There is an NTS visitor centre at Torridon village.

A HORTICULTURAL PARADISE

Between Ullapool and Gairloch is Poolewe, where Inverewe Gardens (above), an NTS property, was created out of almost nothing by Osgood Mackenzie when he took over the house in 1862. He created an unexpected corner of horticultural paradise in the soft, mild west-coast climate, with trees and shrubs from all over the world. By the time of his death in 1922 there were over 2,500 plant species in his garden. The waters of the Gulf Stream, along with successive generations of superb gardening skills, are responsible for what is now one of the major tourist attractions in the north of Scotland.

APPLECROSS

West of Torridon is the Applecross peninsula, facing the islands of Raasay and Skye. A good road, not built until the 1970s, runs round the northern coast of the peninsula from Shieldaig to the village of Applecross, but having come this far it would be a shame not to approach Applecross by the traditional route, through the *Bealach na Ba*, 'the pass of the cattle', on the line of an old drove road. This road rises from sea-level at Kishorn to a height of 2,054ft (626m) within 6 miles (9.5km), with a maximum gradient of 1 in 4 (25 per cent). The final series of hairpin bends approaching the top of the pass at 2,054ft (626m) are an exciting and unforgettable driving experience and certainly not for the faint-hearted. Caravans are not advised – take the long way round to Applecross, through Shieldaig. The viewpoint at the top gives panoramic views of the islands of Raasay and Skye.

The name of the village derives not from a wooden cross made from the wood of an apple tree, but from the Old Gaelic word *apor*, meaning 'at the mouth of' (like *aber*) and *crossain*, 'the little cross', presumably the name of the stream which runs into the sea here. In modern Gaelic the name of the village is *A' Chomaraich*, 'the sanctuary', referring to the 'girth' or extent of monastic sanctuary, said to be 6 miles (9.5km) in all directions. This refers to the monastery founded here in AD673 by St Maelrubha. In early Christian times, before the Norse invaders arrived (after AD800) and laid waste most of the monasteries and churches in the West Highlands, Applecross was an important religious centre, not a sleepy backwater at the end of a tortuous road.

In Loch Maree is *Eilean Ma-Ruibh*, Isle Maree, with a burial ground and a sacred well reported to cure insanity. The patient was dragged around the island, sunwise (clockwise), tied behind a boat and finally put head first into the well. There is still a tree beside this well into which people have driven pennies for luck – and the tree is reportedly dying of copper poisoning. Near Jamestown in Contin is *Preas Ma-Ruibh*, Maelrubha's grove, a sacred grove no doubt of prehistoric origin, as are most of the sacred wells in the Highlands. Also at Contin, and later at Dingwall, an autumn fair, *Feill Ma-Rubha* was held which persisted well into the nineteenth century. The presbytery of Dingwall was scandalised in the seventeenth century to hear of strange pagan practices connected with St Maelrubha. In 1656 the men of Achnashellach were summoned to answer to a charge of sacrificing a bull to 'Mourie' on the saint's day, 25 August, and other 'abominable and heathinishe practizes'. Another complaint was that 'thair wer frequent approaches to some ruinous chappells and circulateing

Left: Burn below Sgurr a'Chaorachain, Applecross, on the twisty road over the Bealach na Ba pass
Pages 68–9: Loch Maree and Slioch

A Saint of The Celtic Church

St Maelrubha (pronounced something like 'mill-ROO-a') was one of the most important and most influential of the early Christian saints, who brought Christianity from Ireland to the northern Picts in the sixth and seventh centuries AD. St Columba of Iona is the best known of these early missionary adventurers – he established the first monastery in AD563, at Iona, and had the good fortune to have his biography (or hagiography) penned by a skilled author, Adomnan. St Maelrubha was not so lucky, but from church dedications we know he was active over a wide area. Because of the vagaries of Gaelic orthography these dedications are often well hidden in place-names – Kilarrow in Islay, far to the south in Argyll, is one example. There, local pronunciation ('killa-ROO') gives the game away. Near Broadford, on Skye, Aisig Mourie or St Maelrubha's Ferry marks the site of a church and burial ground. Churches in Lochcarron, Contin and Ferintosh have connections with St Maelrubha.

Opposite: Victoria Falls near Slattadale on Loch Maree; Queen Victoria visited here in 1877

of them'. If they had been found guilty they would have been 'rebuked in sackcloath' and required to appear publicly at six churches over six Sundays. They chose not to appear. Then in 1678 five Mackenzies of the parish of Gairloch were reported to the presbytery by their minister 'for sacrificing a bull in ane heathnish manner in the iland of St Ruffus, comonlie called Ellan Moury in Lochew for the recovering of the health of Cirstane Mackenzie, who was formerlie sick'. We are not told if the lady recovered her health. This account also mentions a stone, known as Mourie's Stone, which was used for divination. Before undertaking a journey or any new enterprise a person would put his head through a hole in the stone. If there was any difficulty in withdrawing the head this was taken to be a bad omen.

From the *Annals of Tighernac* we learn that in AD673 *Maelruba fundavit ecclesiam Aporcrossan* – Maelrubha founded the church of Aporcrossan (Applecross). We also know that he died there in AD722, on 21 April, at the age of 80 years, 3 months and 19 days, and that he died on a Tuesday. From other sources we learn that before he left Ireland he was Abbot of Bangor and, like Columba, of noble birth. The exact meaning of his name is debated but it is thought that the elements derive from *Mael*, meaning tonsured (as a monk) and Old Gaelic *ruba* (now *rudha*), meaning a point or promontory. This could refer to the place of his birth. Alternatively it could have a more metaphorical meaning, thinking of a missionary monk at the 'cutting edge' of Christianity.

There are various sites around the village of Applecross associated with St Maelrubha. A prehistoric burial cairn is said to be his grave (a common mistake), while west of Applecross House is a holy well, and nearby four trees marking the site of the holy-man's cell. Applecross was second only to Iona in importance as an early monastic centre, and deserves wider recognition.

LOCHALSH

From Kishorn (with the remains of an oil-rig construction yard) the road winds round Loch Carron into Strathcarron and through the village of Lochcarron to Stromeferry, Plockton and Duirinish. Plockton is a pretty, whitewashed village which vies with Eilean Donan castle and Loch Maree for its place on Scottish calendars. It used to be a sleepy fishing and crofting village but is one of many West Highland villages which has adapted to changing times. In summer it is clogged with visitors eager to enjoy its prettiness and its beautiful setting. Most of the population (but not all) are incomers. Most of the houses are holiday homes.

From Plockton it is only a short drive to Kyle of Lochalsh and the new Skye Bridge (1996), with access to the Isle of Skye to the west. The village just across the water is Kyleakin – the name contains a Norwegian king, Haakon. Castle Moil in the village has recently been stabilised.

The pretty village of Plockton, on Loch Carron, looking across to the entrance of Loch Kishorn and the mountains of Applecross

Kyle of Lochalsh is the terminus of the Kyle Line, 82 miles (132km) of scenic railway connecting the west coast to Inverness. The main road to Inverness runs along the coast of Loch Duich, then through Glen Shiel, beneath the Five Sisters of Kintail to Cluanie and thence through Glenmoriston to Invermoriston on Loch Ness, a journey of 55 miles (88km). This is the heartland of the Mackenzie clan. There's lots to explore in Lochalsh and Kintail, and for hill-walkers the long ridge of the Five Sisters is an ambition to fulfill. Not perhaps the combination of danger, exposure and difficulty which makes the Cuillin ridge on Skye such a challenge, but a long and rewarding day nonetheless. The highest of the Five Sisters is Sgurr Fhuaran (3,505ft; 1,068m). On the other side of the main road is the South Cluanie ridge walk with seven peaks over 3,000ft (914m).

Eilean Donan castle at Dornie on Loch Duich is the classic Scottish castle. It's on a little island, connected by an easily defended causeway, with crenellations and slit windows, and it is even floodlit at night. Sean Connery's *Highlander* movie used it as a film set. It seems to be the archtypical Scottish castle. It is, however, a fake.

The Five Sisters of Kintail seen from Mam Ratagan Pass (John Cleare)

Eilean Donan castle was destroyed in 1719 in a codicil to the Jacobite rising of 1715-16 and was left as a ruinous shell. The 'restoration' to its present state was accomplished in the 1930s by the Macrae-Gilstraps as their Highland retreat. The 'castle' is open to the public.

Balmacara House and Gardens are owned by the NTS and are worth a visit. The NTS owns a lot of land in this area – the Balmacara Estate and the Five Sisters of Kintail are NTS properties. In Glen Shiel is a monument to a skirmish which took place there in 1719. Several hundred Spaniards and a few Jacobites under the command of the Marquis of Tullibardine and the Mackenzie chief the Earl of Seaforth landed in Kintail and captured Eilean Donan castle. They were defeated at Glen Shiel by government forces from Inverness under General Joseph Wightman. Eilean Donan was retaken by a naval landing party.

At Cluanie Bridge, if not in a hurry to get back to Inverness, or if heading south for Fort William, it is worth considering the scenic road over to Glen Garry and Invergarry. The view of Loch Garry from the high point of this route is quite superb.

GLENELG

Back at the head of Loch Duich, a side road to the south turns off the main Inverness highway. This is the road to Glenelg, by way of the Mam Ratagan pass. Visitors to Applecross will have had a foretaste of what is in store – a series of sharp hairpin bends, and an ascent to 1,116ft (340m) from sea-level in only 3 miles (5km), with a gradient of 1 in 7. From the viewpoint at the summit there are views back to Loch Duich and Glenshiel, and to the west fine views of the mountains of Skye. Dr Johnson and Boswell crossed this pass on horseback in 1773 on their way to Glenelg. Dr Johnson described it as 'a terrible steep to climb'. Anybody who has ever seen an illustration of the famous lexicographer atop a Highland pony can only sympathise with the pony.

Just before reaching the village of Glenelg is a turn-off for the little ferry across to Kylerhea on Skye – a nostalgic alternative to the Skye Bridge. In Glenelg itself are the remains of the Bernera Barracks, built after the 1715 rebellion to house a government garrison. It is comparable to the Ruthven Barracks at Kingussie. The Glenelg Inn is eighteenth century or earlier and is worth a visit.

Above: Inside the hollow walls of a broch tower a stone staircase gave access to the wallhead, as clearly seen at Dun Troddan

Right: Dun Telve – the ruinous state of the Glenelg brochs allows us to see in cross-section how skilfully these drystone buildings were engineered and constructed

Beyond the village, up Glen Beg, are the two best-preserved mainland brochs in Scotland, Dun Telve and Dun Troddan. Enough remains of each to see something of the engineering and architectural skill involved in their construction. In order to achieve the required height these circular towers

were built with a 'hollow wall' – there is a double wall of drystone masonry with a gallery in between, enclosing stone staircases which allow access to the wall head. Brochs date from the late Iron Age and are thought to have been built in the period 200BC to AD100. Only the brochs at Carloway, on Lewis, and at Mousa in Shetland, are in a better state of preservation. There are so many completely ruined brochs in the Highlands and Islands, some of them just turf-covered mounds, that it is a real treat to see the Glenelg examples.

Beyond Glenelg a single-track road continues 10 miles (16km) around the coast to Arnisdale, on Loch Hourn, 'the loch of hell'. Across the loch is Knoydart. South of Glenelg is Sandaig where Gavin Maxwell lived. He described his experiences with otters there in *Ring of Bright Water*, which was later made into a film.

Thomas Pennant (1726-98) visited Macleod of Arnisdale in August 1772 and tasted Highland hospitality:

I shall never forget the hospitality of the house: before I could utter a denial, three glasses of rum cordialized with jelly of bilberries, were poured into me by the irresistible hand of good Madam Macleod.

Pennant witnessed the herring fishery in full swing, in the upper reaches of Loch Hourn, where he enjoyed:

... an instantaneous and agreeable view of a great fleet of busses [ie small fishing boats], and all the busy apparatus of the herring fishery; with multitudes of little occasional hovels and tents on the shore, for the accommodation of the crews, and of the country people, who resort here at this season to take and sell herrings to the strangers. An unexpected sight, at the distance of thirteen miles from the sea, amidst the wildest scene in nature ...
... in our return from the extremity of this sequestered spot, are most agreeably amused with meeting at least a hundred boats, rowing to the place we were leaving, to lay their nets; while the persons on shore were busied in lighting fires, and preparing a repast for their companions, against their return from their toilsome work.

Encountering these scenes in such a wild and remote place inspired Pennant to philosophy:

So unexpected a prospect of the busy haunt of men and ships in this wild and romantic tract, afforded this agreeable reflection: that there is no part of our dominions so remote, so inhospitable, and so unprofitable, as to deny employ and livelihood to thousands; and that there are no parts so polished, so improved, and so fertile, but which must stoop to receive advantage from the dreary spots they so effectively despise.

HIGHLAND RAILWAYS

The Inverness & Nairn Railway was authorised in 1854 and completed in 1855, bringing the Railway Age to the Highland capital. In August 1858 the Nairn-to-Keith link was completed, joining Inverness to the Great North of Scotland Railway and the growing national network. By 1863 Forres was linked through Grantown to Aviemore and Perth, and direct trains from Inverness to Glasgow, Edinburgh and London became a possibility. The current route over the Slochd to Aviemore was not opened until 1898.

To the north, the line reached Dingwall in 1862 and Invergordon in 1863. The Sutherland & Caithness Railway opened branches to Wick and Thurso in 1874 and was amalgamated with the Highland Railway in 1884.

The effect of railways on Inverness and the Highlands was far reaching. The Highland Railway itself became one of the major industries in Inverness, employing hundreds of men and women. The railways boosted local industries, and created a new industry – tourism. Hotels, guidebooks, tour operators, specialist shops and services – all had to be developed for a new class of visitor. A few local businessmen and property developers made fortunes.

Pages 78–9: Eilean Donan Castle, near Dornie, a 1930s reconstruction of a medieval ruin, looking down Loch Alsh to the Isle of Skye

4 LOCHABER

CIVIL WAR IN SCOTLAND

James Graham, 5th Earl and 1st Marquis of Montrose (1612-50) was appointed King's Lieutenant in Scotland by Charles I in 1644 and immediately proved himself to be a superb military leader, winning six battles in a year, including at Inverlochy, near Fort William. Here, on 2 February 1645 he led a force of 3,000 men, including Irish troops, through the mountains from Fort Augustus to surprise the garrison at Inverlochy, attacking at first light. Over 1,300 men, lowland Covenanters and Campbells under the command of Archibald Campbell, 8th Earl and 1st Marquis of Argyll, were massacred.

Defeated near Selkirk in September 1645, Montrose fled to Norway, but on learning of Charles I's execution in 1649 he returned to Scotland, attempting to raise a force in the Highlands. His force of 300

(continued opposite)

HISTORICALLY THE NAME LOCHABER referred to the district around the head of Loch Linnhe, but through the infelicities of local-government administration the term has come to include all the mainland west of Loch Linnhe and south of Loch Hourn, as well as land to the east of Loch Linnhe down as far as Kinlochleven, Ballachulish and even the north part of Appin. In olden times, Nether Lochaber was the Cameron country south of Ben Nevis, including the Mamores, while Brae Lochaber (or Upper Lochaber) referred to the lands of the MacDonalds of Keppoch.

FORT WILLIAM

Although lying on the eastern side of Loch Linnhe and the Great Glen and so technically outside of the jurisdiction of this book, Fort William is the largest town in Lochaber and its administrative and commercial capital, so it deserves a brief mention here. The town is separated from the foreshore of Loch Linnhe by a rare stretch of dual carriageway, carrying traffic away from the controversial pedestrian mall of the town centre. Thus, at a stroke, the planners destroyed the town's most attractive feature – its lochside character. The population of the Fort William area, including the adjacent settlements of Caol and Corpach, now exceeds 10,000. There is a busy Tourist Information Centre in Fort William.

The original fort was built in 1655 by General Monck, but rebuilt under William III when, for a short time, the town was called Maryborough. Slight traces only of this fort survive. The Jacobites besieged it in 1715 and again in 1745, but failed to capture it. The fort was garrisoned until 1855 and then dismantled. The gateway was re-erected in 1896 at The Craigs, the old cemetery for the town. Some of the seventeenth-century panelling from the former governor's house is preserved in the West Highland Museum. The museum has relics of Bonnie Prince Charlie and the Jacobites as well as archaeological material and a display about the aluminium-processing plant just outside the town. One of the Jacobite exhibits is a secret portrait which is only revealed to be of the prince when a cylindrical mirror is placed on it.

Inverlochy Castle (not to be confused with the five-star hotel of the same name), north of the town, is fifteenth century with later additions. It has circular towers in the corners. The Lord of the Isles won an important skirmish at Inverlochy in 1431, while in 1645 the Marquis of Montrose defeated the covenanters here.

At the head of Loch Linnhe, just to the west of Fort William, the Caledonian Canal reaches the sea at Corpach, descending the eight locks of 'Neptune's Staircase'. Most of the traffic using the canal these days is recreational, though it is still important for the fishing fleet. Linking the three lochs of the Great Glen, Loch Lochy, Loch Oich and Loch Ness, the canal itself is 22 miles long (35km) out of the total 60

(continued)
men was defeated at Carbisdale in April 1650; Montrose sought refuge with Macleod of Assynt at Ardvreck Castle, Sutherland. He was handed over to the authorities for the huge sum of £25,000. By 21 May 1650 Montrose was dead, sentenced to death by the Scottish Parliament without trial, hanged and disembowelled.

Opposite: The Commando Memorial near Spean Bridge, commemorating the men who trained in this area during World War II

Below: Inverlochy Castle, near Fort William

Pages 82–3: The magnificent railway viaduct at Glenfinnan, close to where Prince Charles Edward Stuart raised his standard in the Jacobite rising of 1745–6

miles (96km) of the Great Glen from Fort William to Inverness.

North of Fort William, just outside the village of Spean Bridge, is the Commando Memorial, designed by Scott Sutherland in 1952. This area was used for training during World War II. Achnacarry House, the seat of Cameron of Locheil, was used as a commando headquarters. There is now a small museum of clan history on the estate.

KNOYDART

The peninsula of Knoydart was devastated by the Clearances. Once with a population of 1,000, today a small community of around seventy survives at Inverie, but only a handful were born in Knoydart. The Knoydart Estate consists of 17,000 acres (6,885ha) out of a total of 55,000 acres (22,275ha) for the whole peninsula. Inverie is reached only by small boat from Mallaig. To the north is Loch Hourn and the massive reservoir of Loch Quoich; to the south, Loch Nevis. There is a single-track road to Kinlochhourn. Ladhar Bheinn in Knoydart (3,346ft; 1,020m) is the most westerly 'Munro' on the Scottish mainland.

Repeated emigrations decimated the population of Knoydart, culminating in a major clearance in 1853, when 332 people were taken to Canada on board the *Sillery*, another 60 were evicted and a further 40 threatened with eviction and the destruction of their homes. Yet, the 1861 Census shows a population of nearly 600 remaining. In Denis Rixson's recent study of the history of the peninsula it is estimated that in the 80 years prior to the well-documented and well-publicised clearance of 1853, between 2,000 and 2,500 emigrants left the area. Today the last of the indigenous inhabitants have been dispersed, and only the small community of estate workers and support staff remains.

The last attempt by the native population to achieve a measure of security took place in 1948, when the 'Seven Men of Knoydart' staked a claim to enough land to sustain a reasonable agricultural living – in retrospect, probably an impossibly optimistic dream. A public enquiry was held to investigate the issues, and the land claims dismissed. What made this outcome particularly galling to the local population was that the landowner was Lord Brocket, an extremely right-wing and thoroughly unpleasant character whose views on Nazi Germany in the 1930s were widely regarded as obnoxious.

THE MUNROS

A Munro is the name given to Scottish mountains over 3,000ft (914m), as originally listed by Sir Hugh Thomas Munro (1856-1919) in the first issue of the SMC Journal in 1891. Current lists give 284 Munros.

MOIDART AND MORAR

West from Fort William is 'The Road to the Isles', passing through Glenfinnan and the districts of Moidart and Morar to the end of the road at the fishing port and railhead of Mallaig. It was in Moidart, at Loch nan

Uamh, that Bonnie Prince Charlie landed in 1745; his standard was raised at Glenfinnan on 19 August. There, a monument and an NTS visitor centre commemorate the optimistic beginning of a rebellion which ended disastrously at Culloden in April 1746 – a personal tragedy for Charles Edward Stuart and a social milestone for the people of the Highlands.

The Glenfinnan Monument stands at the head of Loch Shiel, and was erected in 1815 by MacDonald of Glenaladale, a grandson of one of the Prince's original supporters. The Raising of the Standard is remembered each year at an anniversary service. The monument commemorates not Bonnie Prince Charlie but the Highlanders who followed him. Inland from the NTS centre at Glenfinnan is a magnificent railway viaduct, carrying the main line from Fort William to Mallaig. In the summer months, steam trains operate over this line on some services.

The Mallaig road, the last trunk road in the UK which for long stretches is still single-track with passing places, passes the prince's landing place at Loch nan Uamh, where he landed from a French frigate on 5 August 1745. It was perhaps fitting that he left Scotland from the same sheltered inlet on the Sound of Arisaig, on 20 September 1746, five months after the Culloden disaster – five months on the run with a price of £30,000 on his head. He was not betrayed by the people of the Highlands and managed to evade capture from the redcoats of the British army, though he had many narrow squeaks.

The white sands of Arisaig are justly famous, and from several points along this stretch of the 'Road to the Isles' there are wonderful views to the islands of Eigg and Rum, and also northwards to the distant jagged outline of the Cuillins on the Isle of Skye. At the end of this road is Mallaig, with a population of about 900, a small but busy village with shops, hotels and basic services, and a seasonal Tourist Information Centre. The small

KIDNAPPED

The hero of Robert Louis Stevenson's Kidnapped *is David Balfour, who with Alan 'Breck' Stewart, a Jacobite survivor of the Battle of Culloden, dodges the redcoats throughout the hills and glens of the west Highlands before the rebel escapes to exile in France and our hero gains his rightful inheritance at the expense of his wicked uncle. First published in 1886,* Kidnapped *is regarded as a skillful and sympathetic evocation of eighteenth-century Scotland.*

According to tradition, Alan Breck was the Appin Murderer, an army deserter who had changed sides and joined the Jacobite Rising in 1745. The victim was Colin Campbell of Glenure, who on 14 May 1752 was shot and killed in the wood of Lettermore in Appin, south of Ballachulish. Alan Breck was never caught, but James Stewart – 'James of the Glens' – was prosecuted as an accessory to murder, tried by a jury of Campbell lairds at Inveraray and hanged from a gibbet overlooking the narrows at Ballachulish, where his bones, wired together, dangled as a terrible warning for many years.

The identity of the Appin Murderer has never been definitively established, but it was probably not Alan Breck. It seems likely that it must have been somebody important enough to James Stewart that he would hang rather than talk.

Inside the Catholic church at Glenfinnan is a memorial plaque to Bonnie Prince Charlie

A Changed Landscape

The 'wilderness' of Ardgour and Morvern is, like the vast, empty tracts of Sutherland and Knoydart, not 'natural', but the result of over-grazing, a permanent reminder of the combination of economic transformation and human tragedy which created the Highland landscape of today. Here and there are pockets of the original landscape, precious areas of protected woodland in inaccessible gulleys and ravines, on islands and islets too small to be worth grazing.

Pages 86–7: The white sands of Morar at Lon Liath, near Arisaig

Opposite: The castle of Mingary, near Kilchoan in Ardnamurchan, one of the fortresses of the Lords of the Isles

museum located at the railway station is worth a visit and is a good place to buy local books and pamphlets. There is a car ferry from Mallaig to Armadale, on the Isle of Skye, and there are ferry connections to the islands of Rum, Eigg, Muck and Canna, known locally as 'The Small Isles'.

ARDGOUR AND MORVERN

South of the Road to the Isles and on the west side of Loch Linnhe are the districts of Ardgour and Morvern, with the long peninsular finger of Ardnamurchan stretching out to the west. These areas are perhaps best reached by the short ferry crossing of Loch Linnhe at the Corran Narrows, 15 miles (24km) south of Fort William, where a car ferry plies back and forth from early in the morning until late at night.

While passing through Ardgour and Morvern, spare a thought for the population – the ones who are no longer there. These areas too were devastated in the Clearances and emigrations of the nineteenth century, the people replaced by more profitable sheep.

One of the most poignant accounts of the nineteenth-century Clearances is to be found in Rev Norman Macleod's *Reminiscences of a Highland Parish* (1871). One of a dynasty of Macleod divines, he wrote sympathetically from his Morvern manse of the way of life of a people he had grown up with. He records how, as an old woman living in overcrowded housing conditions in Glasgow, Mary Cameron spoke with great emotion and with a clear memory of the day in 1824 when her family was evicted from the township of Unnimore (Inneanmore) in Morvern. She spoke, in Gaelic, of how her husband James carried his mother on his back up the winding trail leading over the hill from Unnimore to the manse near Lochaline. At the top of the hill they paused for a last look back at their modest home, today a roofless ruin. Mary Cameron remembered the pain of that day, and her husband's words: 'We are not afraid. The world is wide, and God will sustain us'.

From Lochaline there is a car ferry to Mull, from where, after a short drive to Craignure, it is possible to connect with a ferry to Oban, the hub of ferry services to the Islands. Passing the manse of Fiunary, where Norman Macleod and his dynasty served the parish of Morvern, the road reaches Drimnin, formerly a Maclean estate. In the north-west corner of Morvern, past Drimnin, and inaccessible by car, is the extensive village of Auliston, now completely deserted but once home to hundreds of people. There are many more settlements like it, scattered throughout the whole length and breadth of the Highlands.

An alternative route from the Corran Ferry leads on to Strontian, a village which has left its mark in the periodic table of elements, for strontium, a deadly by-product of nuclear testing in the 1950s and 1960s, was first identified in the lead mines here. Strontian (the accent is on the

INNER HEBRIDES

The views from Ardnamurchan Point northwards towards the islands of Muck, Eigg and Rum, and westwards to the islands of Coll and Tiree, make the journey along this long and sometimes difficult road well worthwhile. There is no way to hurry on a single-track road, so allow plenty of time for journeys in these remote places. The distances in miles may seem manageable, but travellers have to adjust to unfamiliar conditions.

second syllable) is at the head of Loch Sunart, a particularly beautiful sea loch which penetrates far into the enclosing lands of Morvern and Sunart.

Further to the west, at Salen, the road divides: to the north it winds through the coastal fringes of Moidart to Acharacle, Loch Moidart and Loch Ailort, joining the Fort William-Mallaig road at Kinlochailort; north of Acharacle a side road leads to Castle Tioram (pronounced 'Cheerum'), an important stronghold of the MacDonald Lords of the Isles, probably built in the thirteenth century. It is situated on a rocky islet in Loch Moidart and can be reached on foot at low tide. John, Lord of the Isles in the fourteenth century, left his abandoned wife Amy here, and married a second time to Margaret, daughter of the Stewart who became Robert II, King of Scotland. The Clanranald branch of Clan Donald descends from Amy, and is thus the senior branch of the extensive MacDonald clan. Castle Tioram was occupied and besieged on several occasions but was finally destroyed during the 1715 rising by Allan MacDonald of Clanranald to avoid its occupation by Campbells while he was away supporting the Jacobite cause.

ARDNAMURCHAN

To the west of Salen the road winds along the southern coast of the peninsula of Ardnamurchan, through the village of Kilchoan, ending up at the lighthouse at the Point of Ardnamurchan, the most westerly tip of the mainland of Scotland. There is a summer ferry service from Kilchoan to Tobermory, on Mull.

Near Kilchoan is Mingary Castle, another of the ancient fortresses of the Lords of the Isles. James IV held court there in 1495 and took the submission of the Island chiefs, during his tour of the west coast and Islands. This was designed to stamp royal authority on an area which had been ruled since the 1150s by the MacDonald Lords of the Isles, descendants of Somerlad, who liberated the islands from Norse rule. Mingary was held for them by the MacIans of Ardnamurchan, one of the most powerful branches of Clan Donald. It became a Campbell stronghold in the 1620s but in 1644 was captured for Montrose by Alasdair 'Colkitto' MacDonald (*Coll Ciotach*, 'left-handed Coll'), then recaptured by General Leslie and restored to the Campbells. It was garrisoned during the Jacobite risings and is now in ruins. The enclosure wall probably dates from the thirteenth century.

Few people, and a few more sheep, live in Ardnamurchan, and it is a wild and unforgiving place, except for a few fertile pockets of good land. A geological map of the peninsula reveals that the western end is in fact an extinct volcano, from which igneous dykes radiate out across the landscape in all directions, like the cracks in a pane of glass penetrated by a bullet. But the passage of 65 million years has removed all traces, except to the trained eye, of the cataclysmic events which show up so well and so colourfully on the geologist's maps.

Opposite: Ardnamurchan lighthouse, on the most westerly point of the Scottish mainland

5 LOCH NESS AND THE GREAT GLEN

LOCH NESS AND DRUMNADROCHIT

GLEN ALBYN, THE 'GREAT GLEN' which slices diagonally through the northern part of Scotland, has been since ancient times the main communications route from the west coast to the Moray Firth and the North Sea. It is a geological fault line, perfectly straight, and occupied by a chain of lochs, of which the largest and most famous is Loch Ness. The main road from Fort William to Inverness is much improved, so that it is possible to drive the 66 miles (106km) in 90 minutes, though with summer traffic it is advisable to allow two hours for the journey.

Today the main road keeps to the west side of Loch Ness, but this is a relatively recent development. Historically the track down the east side of the loch was the route north, and when the government ordained that roads should be built throughout the Highlands to connect the major garrisons in the aftermath of the 1715 Jacobite rising, it was on the east side of Loch Ness that General Wade and his successor Major Caulfeild exercised their engineering skills. The road on the west side of Loch Ness was not completed as a suitable route for motor vehicles until the 1930s – and it was soon after this route was opened that the sightings of Nessie started.

Nessie is the Loch Ness Monster, a term coined in 1933 in the columns of the *Inverness Courier*, but soon adopted worldwide. There is a wide spectrum of belief about Nessie, with many true believers (possibly 20,000 people claim to have seen the monster for themselves) and a diminishing hard core of sceptics. What cannot be denied is that many sober, respectable citizens are convinced they have seen something. What is not so easy, is to explain what they have seen. There are many possible explanations, ranging from half-submerged logs to various life forms, including deer, otters, seals, sturgeon and giant eels. The wakes of small boats, often reverberating up and down the loch long after the craft have disappeared from view, are a common explanation. Considerable research has also been done into the effects of winds and currents on the surface of the loch, particularly 'Langmuir Circulations'

Loch Garry from the north shore, in winter (John Cleare)

which are vertical currents reputed to bring bubbles of oxygen bursting to the surface.

Unfortunately various hoaxes, including fake footprints and the most famous photograph of Nessie, the 'Surgeon's Photograph', recently exposed as a fraud, do nothing to encourage belief in the existence of a previously unidentified species. Especially when the exposé itself is condemned as a fraud by true believers. Nessie has been hunted by echo-sounders and the latest electronic technology, by a professional Nessie-hunter, by a miniature submarine, and by an unending stream of eccentrics.

Some of the most interesting recent research has concentrated on calculating the food available in Loch Ness required to support a population of unidentified beasties; the conclusion is that there are insufficient nutrients to support a food chain with large animals at its head. The Nessie phenomenon can be studied in competing exhibitions in the village of Drumnadrochit, half way up the west side of the loch.

Despite modern scepticism, the Nessie story is in fact very old, with the first documented sighting recorded in the biography of St Columba, referring to events during his journey up the Great Glen from Iona to Inverness in the AD580s. According to this account, Columba had to cross the River Ness (not, it should be noted, the Loch) when he came upon a Pictish burial party. They reported that one of their number 'had been seized while swimming by a beast that lived in the water, and bitten very severely'. Sensing a chance to impress, Columba ordered one of his companions to swim across the river to collect a boat for his party. His unfortunate acolyte, Lugne, obeyed orders without delay but had a narrow escape:

But the monster, whose hunger had not been satisfied earlier, was lurking in the depths of the river, keen for more prey. Feeling the water disturbed by his swimming, it suddenly swam to the surface, and with a mighty roar from its gaping mouth it sped towards the man as he swam in midstream.

St Columba intervened just in time, ordering the 'savage beast' to stop, to leave the man alone, and to 'go back with all speed'. It fled, terrified, 'at full speed, as if dragged away by ropes'. The locals were impressed:

The heathen barbarians who were there at the time were impelled by the great power of this miracle, which they had seen with their own eyes, to magnify the God of the Christians.

The idea of strange creatures living in Scottish lochs was commonplace throughout the Highlands and Islands, and part of Celtic folklore. The local populace did not need to convince themselves of the existence of Nessie – their ancestors had believed in such creatures and they did too. Long before the 1933 sighting from the new road popularised Nessie in the press, the locals knew that there was something living in the loch, though something not known to science perhaps. On a hot summer's day in July 1852, the inhabitants of Lochend saw two large objects moving on the loch, and took all the necessary precautions. The men armed themselves with hatchets, the young lads with scythes, and the women with pitchforks. According to the local paper, the *Inverness Courier*, 'one fierce-looking amazon, wielding a tremendous flail about her head, commenced to flagellate a hillock by way of practice'. One old man retrieved an old rifle from his home. The objects turned out in the end to be a couple of ponies from a neighbouring estate, seeking relief from the summer heat by swimming in the loch, but clearly the local people believed that it might have been something else.

So, when planning a journey down this road, allow time to stop in one of the many lay-bys and parking places provided, and don't forget to pack your binoculars and your telephoto lenses.

FORT AUGUSTUS, LOCH OICH AND INVERGARRY

At the south end of Loch Ness is the village of Fort Augustus, another place owing its existence to the military occupation of the Highlands after the Jacobite rising of 1715. The original barracks were replaced by a fort, built by General Wade in 1730 and not finally sold off until 1867, when a

Pages 96–7: Looking north east along Loch Ness (John Cleare)

Below: Woods by Loch Oich, near Laggan, in the Great Glen

95

Benedictine order bought the site and incorporated it into a school and abbey. Both the school and the abbey are now closed, a victim of market forces at the end of the twentieth century. The locks of the Caledonian Canal at Fort Augustus are an attractive place at which to pause and watch the world go by. There is a seasonal Tourist Information Centre in the village.

In one of those ironies which haunt Highland history, Fort Augustus was named after William Augustus, Duke of Cumberland, then a nine-year-old boy. Just sixteen years later he commanded the government troops at Culloden on behalf of his father, King George II, and in the aftermath of that battle he used the fort as a base from which to hunt down Jacobite fugitives. The original name of the settlement which Wade made the hub of his road network in this part of the Highlands was Kilchumein, named after St Chumein. The local secondary school preserves this name in Kilchuimen Academy.

South of Fort Augustus is Loch Oich, and the village of Invergarry, where a monument at the 'Well of the Heads' commemorates one of the more gruesome episodes of Highland history. The bloody heads of seven brothers were washed in this well in 1665, so that the chieftain of the MacDonalds of Keppoch could identify the killers of his two sons. The monument was erected in 1812 and has inscriptions in English, French, Latin and Gaelic.

INVERMORISTON, GLENMORISTON AND URQUHART CASTLE

North of Fort Augustus the road between Fort William and Inverness passes through the village of Invermoriston, from where a side road heads up Glenmoriston and over the watershed to Glen Shiel, Loch Duich, Kyle of Lochalsh and the Isle of Skye.

Between Invermoriston and Drumnadrochit a cairn commemorates John Cobb, who was killed in 1952 while pursuing the world water-speed record in his speedboat. He was well regarded by many local people because he respected the Sabbath during the weeks of preparation for his fatal attempt.

Just south of Drumnadrochit is Urquhart Castle, one of the most important historic sites in the Highlands, as well as one of the most unpronounceable (roughly, 'urr-cart'). The surviving walls owe their ruinous state to events in 1691, when the castle was blown up to prevent its occupation by Jacobites, but underneath them are the remains of a Dark

Opposite: Urquhart Castle on the shores of Loch Ness near Drumnadrochit; a reconstruction of a medieval catapult adds to the atmosphere

Age fortress, possibly visited by St Columba in the AD580s during his foray into the land of the Picts. Some argue that it has a better claim than Craig Phadraig at Inverness as the fort of King Brude of the Picts. The seventeenth-century tower over-looks Urquhart Bay, one of the most popular haunts of the Loch Ness Monster.

The main road north from Drumnadrochit leads directly to Inverness, but it is worth exploring some of the alternatives, for example via Cannich and Strathglass, or over the hill to Kiltarlity and Beauly. One of the finest Scottish glens is Glen Affric, where remnants of the ancient Caledonian pine forest survive. Part of the enchantment of visiting the Highlands is exploring off the beaten track, and the thrill of discovery of all the out-of-the-way places which are not described in guidebooks and tourist literature.

View westwards along Loch Affric with the southern spur of Mam Sodhail in the distance (John Cleare)

USEFUL INFORMATION AND PLACES TO VISIT

TOURIST INFORMATION

Tourist Information Centre, Dornoch
The Square, Dornoch, Sutherland IV25 3SD
Tel: 01862 810400 / 0845 225 5121 Fax:
01862 810644
Accommodation bookings, leaflets, books, maps,
information on bus services, taxis, car hire,
services, events, festivals e.t.c. Open all year.

Tourist Information Centre, Fort William
Cameron Square, Fort William, Inverness-shire
PH33 6AJ
Tel: 01397 703781 Fax: 01397 705184
Accommodation bookings, leaflets, books, maps,
information on bus services, taxis, car hire,
services, events, festivals, yacht charters e.t.c.
Open all year.

Tourist Information Centre, Inverness
Castle Wynd, Inverness, Inverness-shire IV2 3BJ
Tel: 01463 234353 Fax: 01463 710609
Accommodation bookings, leaflets, books, maps,
information on bus services, taxis, car hire,
services, events, festivals e.t.c. Open all year.

Tourist Information Centre, Wick
Whitechapel Road, Wick, Caithness KW1 4EA
Tel: 01955 602596 Fax: 01955 604940
Accommodation bookings, leaflets, books, maps,
information on bus services, taxis, car hire,
services, events, festivals e.t.c. Open all year.

TRAVEL

Caledonian MacBrayne, Mallaig
Ferry Terminal, The Pier, Mallaig,
Inverness-shire PH41 4QB
Tel: 01627 462403 Fax: 01687 462403
Brochure Hotline: 01475 650288
Information on ferry services to Skye (Armadale)
and the Small Isles (Eigg, Muck, Rum, Canna)

Caledonian MacBrayne, Ullapool
Ferry Terminal, Shore Street, Ullapool,
Ross-shire IV26 2YG
Tel: 01854 612358 Fax: 01853 612433
Information on ferry services to Lewis
(Stornaway)

PLACES TO VISIT

Achiltibuie Hydroponcium
Achiltibuie, Ullapool, Ross-shire IV26 2YG
Tel: 01854 622202
Open daily Easter to September 10am to 6pm.
Admission charge for guided tour.

Avoch Heritage Association
Old PO Building, Bridge Street, Avoch,
Ross-shire IV9 8PP
Tel: 01381 621125
Open June to September, Monday to Saturday
11am to 5pm.

A remote track along the shore of Loch Hourn
(John Cleare)

Balmacara Estate and Lochalsh Woodland Garden (National Trust for Scotland)
Lochalsh House, Balmacara, Kyle,
Inverness-shire IV40 8DN
Tel: 01599 566325
Woodland garden open all year daily 9am to sunset. House open 31 March to 30 September daily 9am to 5pm. There is an admission charge for the house.

Balnakeil Craft Village
2 Balnakeil Craft Village, Durness,
Sutherland IV27 4PT
Tel: 01971 511277
Open May to October.

Clan Cameron Museum
Achnaharry, Spean Bridge, Inverness-shire
PH34 4EJ
Tel: 01397 712480 (curator)
Web: www.clan-cameron.org
Open mid-October 1.30pm to 5pm. There is an admission charge.

Cromarty Courthouse Museum
Church Street, Cromarty, Ross-shire IV11 8XA
Tel: 01381 600418
Open Easter to October daily 10am to 5pm. There is an admission charge.

Culloden Moor Visitor Centre (National Trust for Scotland)
Culloden Moor, Inverness, Inverness-shire
IV2 5EU
Tel: 01463 790607
Site open all year. Visitor centre open 1 February to 31 March and 1 November to 31 December daily from 10am to 4pm; 1 April to 31 October daily 9am to 6pm. There is an admission charge for the exhibition.

Dingwall Museum
Town Hall, Dingwall, Ross-shire, IV15 9RY
Tel: 01349 865366
Open mid-May to September, Monday to Saturday 10am to 5pm. There is an admission charge.

Dunrobin Castle
Golspie, Sutherland KW10 6SF
Tel: 01408 633177
Open 1 April to 31 May and 1 to 15 October, Monday to Saturday 10.30am to 4.30pm; 1 June to 30 September, 10.30am to 5.30pm; Sunday, 12 noon to 5.30pm; July and August,10.30am. There is an admission charge.

Eilean Donan Castle
Dornie, by Kyle of Lochalsh, Inverness-shire
IV40 8DX
Tel: 01599 555202
Open March to November daily from 10am to 3pm; Easter to October 10am to 5.30pm. There is an admission charge.

Ferrycroft Countryside Centre
Ferrycroft, Lairg, Sutherland IV27 4TP
Tel: 01549 402160
Open daily April to October. There is no admission charge.

Gairloch Heritage Museum
Achtercairn, Gairloch, Ross-shire IV21 2BP
Tel: 01445 712287
Open April to mid October, Monday to Saturday 10am to 5pm. There is an admission charge.

Glenfinnan Visitor Centre (National Trust for Scotland)
Glenfinnan, Inverness-shire PH37 4LT
Tel: 01397 722250

Site open daily all year. Visitor centre open 1 April to 18 May and 1 September to 31 October, 10 am to 5pm; 19 May to 31 August 9.30am to 6pm. There is an admission charge to the exhibition.

Groam House Museum

High Street, Rosemarkie, Ross-shire IV10 8UF
Tel: 01381 620961
Web: www.groamhouse.org.uk
Open 1 May to 30 September, Monday to Saturday 10 am to 5pm and Sunday 2pm to 4.30pm; 1 October to 30 April, Saturday and Sunday 2pm to 4pm; Easter week daily 2pm to 4.30pm. There is an admission charge in the summer but it does not apply in the winter.

Highland Council Archive

High Inverness Library, Farraline Park, Inverness, Inverness-shire IV1 1NH
Tel: 01463 220330
Open Monday to Thursday, 10am to 1pm and 2pm to 5pm. Write or telephone for an appointment.

Highland Museum of Childhood

Old Victoria Station, Strathpeffer, Ross-shire IV14 9DH, Tel: 01997 421031
Open 1 April to 31 October, Monday to Saturday 10am to 5pm and Sunday 2pm to 5pm; July and August weekdays from 10am to 7pm. There is an admission charge.

Hugh Miller's Cottage (National Trust for Scotland)

Church Street, Cromarty, Ross-shire IV11 8XA
Tel: 01381 600245
Open 1 May to 30 September, Monday to Saturday 11am to 1pm and 2pm to 5pm; Sunday 2pm to 5pm. There is an admission charge.

Inverewe Gardens (National Trust for Scotland)

Poolewe, Ross-shire IV22 8XA
Tel: 01445 781200
Garden open daily 15 March to 31 October 9.30am to 9pm; 1 November to 14 March 9.30am to 5pm. Visitor centre open daily 15 March to 31 October 9.30am to 5.30pm. There is an admission charge.

Inverness Floral Hall

Bught Park, Inverness, Inverness-shire IV3 5SS
Tel: 01463 713553
Open November to early March, daily 10am to 3.30pm; April to October, daily 10am to 6pm. There is an admission charge.

Inverness Library

Farraline Park, Inverness, Inverness-shire IV1 1NH
Tel: 01463 236463
Open Monday and Friday 9am to 7.30pm; Tuesday and Thursday 9am to 6.30pm; Wednesday and Saturday 9am to 5pm.

Inverness Museum and Art Gallery

Castle Wynd, Inverness, Inverness-shire IV2 3EB
Tel: 01463 237114
Open all year, Monday to Saturday 9am to 5pm. There is no admission charge.

Mallaig heritage Centre

Station Road, Mallaig, Inverness-shire PH41 4PY
Tel: 01687 462085
Open April to October, Monday to Saturday 11am to 4pm; May to September, also Sunday 1pm to 4pm; longer hours in July and August. There is an admission charge.

Mallaig Heritage Centre
Station Road, Mallaig
Inverness-shire PH41 4PY
Tel: 016987 462085
Open April to October Monday to Saturday 11am to
    4pm; May to September also Sunday 1pm to 4pm;
    longer hours July and August
Admission charge

Official Loch Ness Monster Exhibition
Drumnadrochit
Inverness-shire IV63 6TU
Tel: 01456 450573
Open daily all year, hours vary
Admission charge to exhibition

Original Loch Ness Monster Exhibition
Drumnadrochit
Inverness-shire IV63 6TU
Tel: 01456 450342/450225
Open daily all year, hours vary
Admission charge to exhibition

National Trust for Scotland Countryside Centre
Torridon, Achnasheen
Ross-shire IV22 2EZ
Tel: 01445 791221
Open 1 May to 30 September Monday to Saturday
    10am to 5pm; Sunday 2pm to 5pm
Admission charge

Strathnaver Museum
Bettyhill, by Thurso
Sutherland KW14 7SS
Tel: 01641 521418
Open April to October 10am to 1pm and
    2pm to 5pm
Admission charge

Tain Through Time
Tower Street, Tain
Ross-shire IV19 2DY
Tel: 01862 894089
Open mid March to October daily 10am to 6pm
Admission charge

Timespan Heritage Centre
Dunrobin Street, Helmsdale
Sutherland KW8 6JX
Tel: 01431 821327
Open April to mid October Monday to Saturday
    9.30am to 5pm; Sunday 2pm to 5pm (6pm during
    July and August)
Admission charge

Ullapool Museum and Visitor Centre
7 & 8 West Argyle Street, Ullapool
Ross-shire IV26 2TY
Tel: 01854 612987
Open November to March Wednesday and Saturday
    11am to 3pm; April to October Monday to
    Saturday 9.30am to 5.30pm
Admission charge

UKAEA Exhibition Centre
Dounreay, Thurso
Caithness KW14 7UA
Tel: 01847 802572/802701
Open 3 May to 29 October daily 10am to 4pm
Free admission

Urquhart Castle
Nr Drumnadrochit
Inverness-shire IV63 2XJ
Tel: 01456 450551
Open daily October to March 9.30 am to 4pm (last
    admission); April to September 9.30am to 5.45pm
    (last admission)
Admission charge

West Highland Museum
Cameron Square, Fort William
Inverness-shire PH33 6AJ
Tel: 01397 702169
Open October to May Monday to Saturday 10am to
    4pm; June to September 10am to 5pm; July and
    August also Sunday 2pm to 5pm
Admission charge

PLACE-NAMES AND THEIR MEANINGS

(G, Gaelic; OG, Old Gaelic; N, Norse; ON, Old Norse; P, Pictish; W, Welsh)

Place-name	Derivation	Meaning
Acharacle	*a' Thorkill* (N)	the river of Torquil (Norse personal name derived from 'Thor's kettle')
Achnasheen	*achadh na sin* (G)	field of storm
Affric, Glen	*ath bhraich* (G); or *ath breac* (G)	ford of the boar; or speckled ford
Alligin, Beinn	*ailleag* (G)	jewel, pretty woman
Alness	*ailean* (G) + *-ais* (P)	of the green plain
Alsh, Loch	*loch aillse* (G)	fairy loch
Altnaharra	*allt na h-eirbhe* (G)	stream with the stone-and-turf fence
Applecross	*apor crossain* (OG)	at the mouth of the little cross stream
Ardgour	*ard gobhar* (G)	height of the goat
Ardnamurchan	*ard na muirchun* (G)	point of the otter
Arisaig	*ar oss* (N) + *aig* (G)	river's mouth bay
Arkle	*ark-fjall* (N)	ark mountain
Arnisdale	*Arnis dal-r* (N)	dale of Arni, a Viking
Assynt	*asynt* (ON); or *ass endi* (N)	seen from afar; ridge end
Auliston Point	*rudha nan amhlaistean* (G); or *Olafstein* (N)	point of the troubles; or Olaf's rock
Aultbea	*allt beath* (G)	stream with birches
Avoch	*abh-ach* (G)	river place
Badachro	*bad a'chrotha* (G)	clump at the fold
Balintore	*baile an todhair* (G)	bleaching village (flax)
Balmacara	*baile mac Carra* (G)	village of the sons of Carra or Ara
Balnakill	*baile na chille* (G)	township of the church
Bernara	*Bjarnarey* (N)	Bjorn's island
Bettyhill	after Elizabeth, Countess of Sutherland, c.1820	
Black Isle	*eilean dubh* (G)	black island
Bonar Bridge	*am bonnath* (G)	the bottom ford
Broom, Loch	*braon* (G)	drizzling rain, dew
Brora	*bru-r a* (ON)	bridge river
Caithness	*cataibh* (G) + *nes* (ON)	ness (headland) of the 'Cat-people'
Canisp	*kenna ups* (ON)	well-known house roof (from its shape)
Canna	*kanna-ay* (ON)	pot-shaped island
Cannich	*cannach* (G)	myrtle
Clachtoll	*an clach thuill* (G)	the split rock (on the beach there)
Cluanie	*claon* (G)	a slope
Cromarty	*crom airde* (G)	crooked height
Culloden	*cul lodain* (G)	at the back of the little pool
Dingwall	*thing voll-r* (ON)	assembly meeting place
Dornie	*dornach* (G)	pebble place
Dornoch	*dornach* (G)	pebble place
Dounreay	*dun reidh* (G)	smooth hill
Drimnin	*druinnein* (G)	little ridge (diminutive of dronn)

Place-name	Derivation	Meaning
Drumnadrochit	*druim na drochaid* (G)	ridge of the bridge
Duich, Loch	*Dubhthaich* (G); or *dubh fhaich* (G)	of St Duthac; or dark field
Dunnet	*dun* (G) + *hofud* (ON)	hill-headland
Dunrobin	*druim rabhainn* (G)	hill ridge with the long grass (*druim* and *dun* are often confused in place-names)
Durness	*dyr nes* (ON)	deer promontory
Earradale	*eyrar dalr* (N)	gravelly valley (from the beach)
Eddrachilis	*eadar a' chaoilais* (G)	between the straits (kyles)
Eigg	*eag* or *eige* (G)	the nick (notch)
Embo	*Eyvind-bol* (ON)	Eyvind's place (farm)
Eriboll, Loch	*earbil* (G) from *eyri-bol* (ON)	place on the gravelly bank
Evanton	after Evan Fraser of Balcony, c. 1800	
Ewe, Isle of	*eugh* or *eubh* (G); or *eo* (Irish)	an echo, cry; or yew tree
Foinaven	*foinne bheinn* (G)	wart mountain (it has three protuberances)
Fort Augustus	after William Augustus, Duke of Cumberland; named by General Wade, 1730	
Fortrose	*foter rois* (G)	beneath the promontory
Gairloch	*gear loch* (G)	the short loch
Garry, Glen	*garbh* (G); or *garidh* (G)	rough; or a copse, rough place
Garve	*garbh* (G)	rough
Glasven	*glas bheinn* (G)	green mountain
Glenelg	*Eilg* (G)	the glen of a man Eilg, 'the noble'
Glenfinnan	*gleann Fingon* (G)	glen of Fingon (cf Mackinnon)
Golspie	*Gold's-bol* (ON)	Gold's place, ie farm (from a Norse personal name)
Gruinard	*grunn-fjord* (N); or *groenn-fjord* (ON)	shallow bay (in Gaelic the 'f' is aspirated and so disappears); or green bay
Helmsdale	*hjalm-r dalr* (ON); or *Hjalmunds-dal-r* (ON)	valley of the helmet; or Hjalmund's dale
Hilton of Cadboll	kott-r bol (ON)	place of wild cats
Hope, Ben	hop (ON)	valley among hills
Hourn, Loch	sorn, suirn (G)	a kiln, so 'furnace-shaped', hellish
Inchnadamph	*innis na damh* (G)	pasture of the ox
Inverbreckie	*breac* (G)	speckled (former name of Invergordon)
Invergarry	*garbh* (G)	rough
Invergordon	from Sir Alexander Gordon, c. 1760	
Inverkirkaig	*inbhir* (G) + *kirkiu-vagr* (ON)	at the mouth of the church-bay
Invermoriston	*mor easan*	the big waterfall
Inverness	*inbhir* (G) + *Nesa* (P)	at the mouth of the Ness river

Place-name	Derivation	Meaning
Kilchoan	*cill Comhghain*	church of St Congan
Kildonan	*cill Donan* (G)	church of St Donan
Kinlochbervie	*ceann loch* (G) + *bior* (OG) or *berwi* (W)	the head of the loch of the bubbling spring
Kintail	*ceann t'saile* (G)	at the head of the salt water
Kishorn	*keis horn* (N)	bulky cape
Knoydart	*cnut-fjord* (N)	fjord of Cnut
Kylerhea	*caol Reathainn* (G)	sound of Reathainn, of the Feinn
Kylesku	*caolas cumhann* (G)	narrow strait
Lairg	*learg* (G)	a plain
Laxford Bridge	*lax-fjord* (ON)	salmon bay
Lochaline	*aluinn* (G)	very fair, lovely
Loyal, Ben	*laghail* (G) from *laga-vollr* (ON)	law field
Lybster	*hliebolstadr* (ON)	shelter place
Mallaig	*ma-r/mall* (N) + *aig* (G) from *vik* (N)	bay of seagulls, maws (mews)
Maree, Loch	*Maolrubha* (G)	Irish saint
Melness	*mel-r nes* (ON)	sandy cape
Moidart	*Mundi* (G) + *fjord* (N)	Mundi's fjord
Morar	*mor dhobar* (G)	big water
Moriston, Glen	*mor easan* (G)	the big waterfall
Morven	*mor bheinn* (G)	the big ben (mountain)
Morvern	*mor bhearna* (G)	big passes, big cleft
Muck	*eilean muc* (G)	island of pigs
Oldshoremore	*fhas thir* (G)	productive land (corruption of Ashir)
Opinan	*na h'obainean* (G)	the little bay
Ord, The	*ord* (G)	steep, rounded height
Plockton	*am ploc* (G)	a large turf
Quinag	*cuinneag* (G)	churn, milk pail (from its shape)
Rhiconich	*rudha coinnich* (G)	point covered with moss (or fog)
Rosemarkie	*ros maircnidh, marcanaidh* (G)	promontory of the house-burn
Rum	*rum or ruim* (G); or *rym-r* (N)	place or space; or a roaring (from its waterfalls)
Scourie	*skogr* (ON) + *airigh* (G)	wood shieling
Shandwick	*sand-vik* (ON)	sandy bay
Shiel, Glen	*skjold-r* (ON)	sheltered glen
Shieldaig	*skjold-r* (N) + *aig* (G); or *sild* (N) + *aig* (G) fr *vik* (N)	sheltering (shielded) bay; or herring bay
Shin, Loch	*sian* (ON)	a charm – loch of the charm
Stac Pollaidh	*stac* (G) from *stak* (ON) + *pollaidh* (G)	stack pool
Strathcarron	*srath car abhuin* (G)	valley of the winding river
Strathnaver	*stranar* (G) from *nabho* (Celtic)	divided valley

Place-name	Derivation	Meaning
Strath Oykell	*uchel* (British)	high valley (cf Ochil)
Strathpeffer	*srath pheofhair* (G)	beautiful valley (cf Welsh *pefr*)
Strome Ferry	*straum-r* (ON)	stream (or current)
Strontian	*sron tiahhain* (G)	cape with the little hill
Suilven	*suil bheinn* (G); or	eye-like hill (or 'prospect hill');
	sul-r (ON)	or a pillar
Sunart, Loch	*Sweyn-fjord* (N)	fjord of Sween (Suanus, Sueno)
Sutherland	*sudrland* (ON)	southern land
Sutors of Cromarty	*na Sudraichean* (G)	the tanneries, but influenced by Scots *sutor*, a shoemaker
Tain	*teinn* (ON)	twig, osier
Thurso	*thjorsa-a* (ON)	bull's river
Tioram, Castle	*tioram* (G)	dry, without moisture
Tomnahurich	*tom na h'iubhraich* (G)	yew-tree hillock
Tongue	*tange* (ON)	a tongue or spit of land
Torridon	*torr bheartan* (G)	place of portage
Ullapool	*Olaf-bol* (ON)	Olaf's place (farm)
Wick	vik (ON)	a bay
Wrath, Cape	hvarf (ON)	a turning (out of sight)

FURTHER READING

Darling, Sir Frank Fraser and Boyd, J. Morton. *The highlands and islands*. London: Collins, 1989

Darling, Sir, Frank Fraser. *West Highland survey : an essay in human ecology*. London: Oxford University Press, 1955

Donovan, Kenneth (ed). *The island: new perspectives on Cape Breton's history*, 1713-1990 (UCCB Press, 1990)

Gifford, John. *Highland and Islands*. Harmondsworth: Penguin in association with the Buildings of Scotland Trust, 1992

Humphreys, Rob. *Scottish Highlands & Islands: the Rough Guide*. London: Rough Guides, 2000

Hunter, James. *Last of the Free: a millennial history of the Highlands and Islands of Scotland*. Edinburgh: Mainstream, 2000

Hunter, James. *The making of the crofting community*. New ed. Edinburgh: John Donald, 2000

Miers, Richenda. *Scotland's highlands and islands*. London: Cadogan Books, 1998

Noble, Robin. *North and West: a discovery of the landscape of the North and West Highlands of Scotland*. Dalkeith: Scottish Cultural Press, 2000

Prebble, John. *The Highland Clearances*. Harmondsworth: Penguin, 1969

INDEX

Page numbers in *italics* indicate illustrations

ACKNOWLEDGEMENTS

Many thanks to the staff of Inverness Public Library, for their assistance in
researching this book, particularly the staff of the Reference Room;
to Sue Skelton, for help in listing museums and heritage centres in a sector which is
constantly expanding and changing; to the Highlands of Scotland Tourist Board;
to Derek Croucher for his superb photography;
and to Sue Viccars for her dedicated editorial control.
The poem Characteristics on page 54 is from Norman MacCaig's Collected Poems
© Norman MacCaig 1985, published by Chatto & Windus.